Truth and Meaning

Sam Guinness

CONTENTS

INTRODUCTION

This collection of essays was written in response to an epistemological crisis. I am an Englishman born to a country in need of the church but failed by its spiritual and philosophical doctrine. Britain is the home of the English language. Britain's famous families, characters, folk tales, songs and literature are the contents of the world's language games. English is the internet's mother tongue and thus the English language is this country's greatest export. For Britain to realise its greatness it must start to offer the world a sense of meaning about our existence. This collection of essays attempts to offer just that.

From a very early age, I had played the position of knowledge maker. I had taken the position that when I am ignorant of something the likelihood is the rest of my peers and my community will be too. I was the luckiest child on the planet for 19 years, and yet the church, the school and the family had not offered answers to the most fundamental questions of our existence. In the face of personal suffering, moral cowardice and societal ignorance I started to read voraciously and had the misfortune, honour and responsibility of trying to solve some of our society's most important questions.

My subjective epistemological crises coincided with political and social disaster throughout western liberal democracy. In 2016 Britain made the shock decision to leave the European Union. Following the Syrian Refugee crisis of 5 million migrants, the far right became prominent all around Europe for the first time since the end of World War Two. In America, they elected Donald Trump as President, an individual who in character and policy repeatedly threatened to destroy American democracy and enable far right movements throughout the world.

As one of the first generations to be born to the internet, I started to write to help conceptualise the unique sociological, cultural and technological powers that were conditioning our community. At the LSE, I studied with the world's leading academics on the social sciences of the internet. Very often I was communicating and making sense of ideas that had never been written about elsewhere. In part, this was because of my experiences growing up with the internet, partly my academic training and partly my fatal attraction towards the truth. My investigations on digital violence, cyberstalking and phone hacking have been my greatest contributions to the discourse and are proving to be some of the 21st century's greatest problems.

In 2019 I started to write about the cultural subjects that had defined my life. The result of these essays provided the foundation for a biographical introspection of self using the heuristic weaponry of Christopher Hitchens, George Orwell, Sam Harris, Edward Said, Louis Theroux and Thomas Piketty. In 2020 I offered evidence to the Law Commission on the state of Digital Coercive Control. This speech contributed toward an amendment to the Online Harms Bill, aside from Brexit, arguably the most significant piece of social legislation since the creation of the internet.

Involvement with efforts to stop the re-election of Donald Trump, media monitoring of the Coronavirus and working with Extinction Rebellion, the world's largest non-violent direct action climate movement, led to a great deal of learning and produced knowledge and essays that are contained in this collection.

These 25 essays relay the subjective experience of growing up in London, my adventures at the University of Bristol, my experiences as a musician, specialising in the subject of the fourth industrial revolution whilst studying at the LSE, my journey learning to master and teach meditation, my efforts working with the world's largest non-violent direct action climate movement, my falling in love with film, my investigations into the state of cyber violence and my efforts at preventing far right populism.

I have found intellectual cowardice to be one of the most harmful and extraordinary features of our existence on this planet. I have constantly used my essays as the antidote towards these societal ills. Aesthetically I think the truth is the most beautiful thing on earth and will sacrifice great deals in the pursuit of it. These essays are the sum of the most beautiful ideas that I have found.

CHELSEA FOOTBALL CLUB

Living in Putney and supporting Chelsea Football Club felt like joining the Free Masons. Through virtue of pledging your social, emotional and sporting energy towards Chelsea you were instantly loved by a host of adults. Through virtue of following Chelsea one always had something to talk about with men and boys. Through loving Chelsea me and my friends created a series of living heroes that were willing to fight on our behalf just a mile away from where we lived. Through Chelsea, I learnt loyalty and competition. Through Chelsea, I learnt strategy and style.

My brother is 6 years older than me which is a large difference in the first stages of life where he was inevitably learning and experiencing completely different things to myself. Watching football and playing football related video games became the platform through which I had the ability to spend time with him. I benefitted from the videos that he had spent hours watching. As a child, I had two favourite VHS cassettes that I would watch as much as possible, both of which were concerned with strength, power and victory. They were the Lion King and the Chelsea 1996/1997 season where Chelsea beat Middlesborough at the old Wembley after an incredible first minute strike from Di Matteo and a Gianfranco Zola assisted Eddie Newton goal at the 83rd minute.

During primary school football had the ability to make up the entirety of our non-education lives. At playtime, you would play football. After school, I would spend evenings playing football and FIFA. On Friday I would play 5 A Side football. On Saturday and Sunday, I would watch football and play FIFA. Every day would be accompanied with a constant commentary about experiences of watching and playing football.

From a very early age, my Godbrother and I got massively into football shirts. A football shirt was the greatest symbol that one might acquire. A Chelsea shirt with Lampard or Zola on the back put me one step closer to feeling that I was Lampard or Zola. On holidays in European capitals, we would collect shirts from sports shops and flea markets. In Spain I bought a bootleg Raul shirt, which was then sported playing football in the town square amongst the wine and Al Fresco dining. In Rome when I was just 7 I acquired the gorgeous blue and black striped Pirelli Inter Milan shirt. Walking through the streets of Rome, a city dominated by the football clubs of Roma and Lazio, men would celebrate me shouting 'INTAAA' and rustle the buzz cut I sported because it made me better at heading the football. In Paris I bought a Red and White Lyon shirt from the Les Halles Metro. In a Barcelona market, I bought an impeccably beautiful teal Barcelona shirt sponsored by Unicef. In South Africa, I bought a blue and white striped Mamelodi Sundowns shirt. These shirts were practical, well designed and the most authentic representation of the spaces that you visited because very often football shirts weren't available beyond the given country.

My romantic imagination of Chelsea Football Club was stimulated from a very early age thanks to a Michael Morpurgo book about a Chelsea Pensioner called Billy who plays for Chelsea Football Club before fighting in World War One. He gets good at football through practising with a tennis ball, a technique I tried for a brief period of time. Beyond this fantastic book, a must for all children who like football, excitement and imagination of Chelsea football club is stimulated through the songs. The 1996/1997 video was particularly significant because it featured the music video of Blue Day, a song written by no other than Madness' Suggsy in support of the 1997 FA Cup Final. At the age of 4, 5 or 6 I recognised Suggsy, one of Mod subculture's greatest heroes, as an elder and ally, who, through virtue of supporting Chelsea might well support me. His West London folk tale sung in chorus with Dennis Wise, Gianfranco Zola, Gianluca Vialli and Ruud Gullit confirmed that supporting Chelsea, with Stamford Bridge being 'the only place to be every other Saturday', would forever be an enjoyable partner.

Spectating football matches is one of the best ways to be mindful of the seasons. No other activity demands that someone sits or stands outside for 2 hours. One cannot help but breathe, sense and smell the difference between autumn sunshine, winter darkness and spring heat and there is no better place to observe this than when singing inside Stamford Bridge.

Through attending games, one became acquainted with songs that seemed to have a historical resonance, as if they had been sung in chorus with thousands of strangers decades before me. Carefree, One Man Went To Moe, Chelsay, Chelsay, Chelsaaaaaaay, Chelsay, Chelsay Chelsay CHELSAY!, STAMFORD BRIDGE TOO WEMBERLAY, cellaray, cellaray, Super Frank, Oh Dennis Wiiiiiiiiiiiiise Scored A Fucking Great Goooooooooal At the San Sirooooooooo, VEEALEE, VEEALEE VEALLEE, Darbul Darbul Darbul, Bluuuu Is the Culaaaa, Stan Up If You Ate Totnem, Sit Dan If You Ate Totnem, We Hate Totnem, Hooooosay Moureeeenioooo Hooooosay Moureeeeenio (sang to Verdi's Rigoletto), We're Ownly Ere for tha Pidgeon, Who Are Ya, We Forgot That You Were Ere, We Sirport Are Local Team, We'll just call you Dave, We needasong for Ramirez.

Being present when these songs get created or learnt is an incredible thing. In 2011 I attended Torres' second match away against Fulham, at which we all learnt the words, 'he used to go out on the rob and now he's got a proper job, Fernando Torres Chelsea's Number 9', sung to the tune of The Clash's English Civil War. In 2013, I was ball boying for Frank Lampard's 200th goal, which then led to a song from the Matthew Harding Lower.

My first Chelsea games were against Newcastle and then Sunderland in 2002. We won both games 3-0 with Gallas, Desailly, Hasslebaink, Gudsjohnsen and Zola amongst the scorers. Claudio Ranieri's Chelsea complete the season in 4th achieving qualification to the Champions League. In the Summer, we were bought by a little known Russian billionaire named Roman Abramovich. Every time we bought *The Mirror* Chelsea had bought another player. We spent £111.8 million pounds bringing in Johnson, Geremi, Bridge, Duff, Cole, Veron, Mutu, Crespo and Makelele. It was like some kind of glorious hack on FIFA that allowed a Chelsea fan to buy whoever he wanted. And then, in 2004, Britain's equivalent of the Beatles' 1964 invasion of America happened, Jose Mourinho arrived in London telling the press 'I have to say this, we have top players. I am sorry if I am a bit arrogant, we have a top manager. I am European champion, I am not one of the bottle. I think I am the special one'. Mourinho added Cech, Drogba and Carvalho and Chelsea won the league almost a century after their first victory.

Jose Mourinho laid the foundation for the Chelsea team that would accompany me through secondary school. This squad belonged to my generation. Between 2006 and 2012 Chelsea won the Premier League twice, the FA Cup four times, the League cup once, the Europa League once and the Champions League once. We had 7 managers in 8 years. This turbulence may have proved fatal for many football teams, yet, Chelsea's infrastructure of success was built on the fact we had five first team players, John Terry, Frank Lampard, Didier Drogba, Ashley Cole and Petr Chech, that could act as captain. These men understood the game better than most and had the experience and discipline needed to lead and win. If one of them was fit, Chelsea had a captain with the ability to lead 11 men on and off the pitch. If all of them were fit we had one of the strongest footballing teams in the world. After hundreds of millions of pounds of investment, a club can lose its identity. The fact that three of Chelsea's best players were Londoners was of central importance towards leading the club because not only did they understand the significance of playing in the English league but they also understood the significance of playing in London. As a child, I had dreamed of becoming a Chelsea Footballer. When shaving my head or playing with a tennis ball or getting Zola on my shirt, it wasn't just a posture.

I actually believed that my actions may make me more likely to become a Chelsea footballer. I am certain that thousands of other Chelsea fans had the exact same dreams. With John Terry, Frank Lampard and Ashley Cole we were viewing the realisation of our desires and the extension of our selves, demonstrating that London could create three lads that had the ability and talent to guide 11 football players, Putney, South London and West London, through the Premier League and to Europe.

The 2006 Chelsea squad evolved and improved at the same time as I was doing the exact same through secondary school. Together we all got stronger, taller and smarter. Yet, amidst the hegemony and footballing dominance, the Champions League had always alluded us. Champions League knockout games were being won and lost amidst controversy and drama. In 2003/4 I had witnessed the greatest game of my life when Chelsea won 4-2 against Barcelona, a match so tense it had merited a 9 year old to shout 'FUCK' following Ronaldinho's toe-poke into the right side of the Chelsea goal. The semi-final was then lost against Monaco. In 2004/5 we lost to a contentious Luis Garcia 'ghost goal'. In 2006/2007 we lost once again to Liverpool on penalties in the Semi Final. In 2007/08 we lost against Manchester United in the Final after Terry slipped when taking the deciding penalty. In 2008/09 year Chelsea was knocked out in the semi-finals by a last minute goal from Barcelona's Iniesta following the denial of three credible penalty appeals.

In 2012, after 6 years of exploring the cities of Europe in stadiums like the Nou Camp, the Allianz Arena, Estadio do Dragao and the Donbass Arena, Chelsea fans had felt as if we had played the football that deserved the Champions League trophy. Forget football, Chelsea fans had felt pretty much every emotion that one can evoke through the canon of English literature. The sense of injustice could be felt through every molecule of Stamford Bridge. In 2012, Chelsea's infrastructure of success was terminating. At the end of the year, Frank Lampard would be 34, John Terry 32, Ashley Cole 32, Didier Drogba 34 and Petr Cech 30. We had the sense that the class of Jose Mourinho wouldn't achieve the greatness they deserved and we would never have the opportunity to meet the fate prophesied in the playground, the pubs, the telly studios and the North, East, South and West stand.

It is my greatest pride as a football fan that I attended every Chelsea home game of the 2011/2012 Champions League.

After drawing away at Valencia and Genk and losing to Bayern Leverkusen, Chelsea needed victory in their final match against Valencia to ensure they got through to the knockout stages. Anyone that was at Stamford Bridge for the final group stage match against Valencia felt that the stadium had a strange electric energy about it. Very often one hears about how the inexperience of footballers subdues the performance. Seldom do we hear about how the inexperience of football fans influences the energy on the pitch. I'm not surprised that Anfield, a stadium in a city of just 900,000 people, is a fortress for European football. They have generations of fans with experience of hosting European football clubs and getting good results. After 9 years of excitement and controversy, Chelsea fans knew that they needed self-control and energy to enhance the club's prospect of victory. We had to offer the same discipline and ambition that we had seen from our players. Two Drogba goals bought Chelsea to a 3-0 victory over Valencia and allowed us to progress to the knockout stages.

Even as Chelsea fans got used to new managers this didn't mean we liked the instability. The loss of Mourinho after assembling the infrastructure of Chelsea's long term success and winning the title twice after a century without was idiotic. The loss of Grant and Scolari did not impact the fans. The unavailability of Guus Hiddink certainly did. The worst decision the club made was removing Carlo Ancelotti after he won the Premier League and FA Cup in his first season and then narrowly lost the Premier League title to Manchester United the following season. Chelsea had looked strong and fast and Ancelotti had the experience to make the most of an incredible group of players and establish Chelsea as a footballing institution that might, over the years, consistently build squads and bring players through the academy. Ancelotti was removed just two hours after taking Chelsea to second in the Premier League. Chelsea had lost one of the greatest managers in Football, failing the fans and the players. The sense of waste wasn't helped by rumours that he had been sacked because of Torres' bad form.

Ancelotti's replacement Andres Villas Boas failed Chelsea's players. The worst game I've ever seen Chelsea play was the 5-3 loss to Arsenal where AVB's infamous highline left extraordinary amounts of space for the pace of Theo Walcott and the incredible form of Robin Van Persie. In Naples, for the first leg of the round of 16, Ezequiel Lavezzi and Edison Cavani tore apart Chelsea just as Walcott and Van Persie had. Chelsea lost 3-1 and Andres Villas-Boas was sacked. Roberto Di Matteo, the star of that 1996/1997 FA Cup Final VHS, would be Chelsea's replacement manager for the 2012 season, giving him the task of overturning the 3-1 loss to Naples.

Chelsea changed managers so often that one could never be sure of how good their memory of the Football club was. Even after mastering the Football club academically, they almost certainly didn't have the phenomenological experience of being with Chelsea for the last decade. Thankfully, on match day, we had the memories of John Terry, Frank Lampard, Ashley Cole, Petr Cech and Didier Drogba who were completely aware of the significance of Chelsea's position in the Premier and Champions League and of greatest importance, we had the collective memory of 40,000 Chelsea fans who attended the matches. No fan would ever forget the raw phenomenological experience of what it had felt like to lose against Barcelona, Liverpool or Manchester United. Every fan knew what the Champions League meant to that squad of Chelsea players and we would use noise to ensure we won.

Sat left of the lower Matthew Harding stand, Chelsea's 4-1 victory over Napoli is the greatest game of football I've ever seen. Imagine 120 minutes of 40,000 hunter gatherers totally wired towards finding the goals that would overturn 6 years of injustice. Excellent headed goals from Drogba, Terry, a penalty from Lampard and an extra time goal from Ivanovic took Chelsea through to the Quarter Finals. Now imagine 40,000 ravenous minds synthesised in sweet harmony on Madness' One Step Beyond. It had been our infrastructure of leadership and the memory of 40,000 fans that had caused one of Chelsea's greatest comebacks.

We would then play the Portuguese side Benfica in the Quarter Finals of the Champions League. We played two games after Napoli, losing 2-1 to Manchester City and drawing 0-0 to Tottenham. We won the Quarter Final 3–1 on aggregate with an excellent last-minute goal from Raul Merrieles, leading to a rematch with our Champions League rivals Barcelona.

Barcelona hated playing Chelsea. Messi had never scored against us. They hated the size of Stamford Bridge, the fans much closer, the pitch much smaller. They had been beaten 4-2 in 2004 and knew that they were lucky to have won the tie in 2009. Chelsea's 1-0 victory over Barcelona in the first leg of the Champions League final was a battle of attrition. Everything about Barcelona's team suggests Chelsea shouldn't have won that match. This was the Guardiola team of Messi, Fabregas, Xavi, Iniesta, Puyol and Fabregas. They were arguably the greatest side in modern Football, winning the La Liga, the Champions League and many of them the 2010 World Cup. Fabregas was cleared off the line. Sanchez failed to shoot after being chipped through on goal by Messi. Pedro hit the post. Chelsea had one chance. Drogba scored.

Going into the away tie, we were all aware that Barcelona were going to outplay us. We had seen Chelsea's rubbish performances in the League and we were completely outplayed, and yet, this was Chelsea in the Champions League. This was Cech, Cole, Terry, Lampard and Drogba. No one expected that 1 nil down and missing Gary Cahill after an 11th-minute injury that John

Terry, Chelsea's most experienced defender and the one footballer who made it good through our academy, would get himself sent off for unnecessarily kneeing Sanchez in the back. Chelsea had three defenders, Boswinga, Ivanovic and Ashley Cole, against the greatest attacking side of the 21st century. We went 2-0 down and then out of nowhere, just before halftime, Ramires scored Chelsea's goal of the Season, looping the ball over Valdez after Lampard's through ball. 2-2 on aggregate, the additional away goal would be all we needed to go through to the Champions League Final.

In the second half, we had 9 footballers in lines guarding the penalty box blocking and barging Football's most skilful players. Once again, a fatal mistake from one of our leaders. Drogba's lunge took down Fabregas. Messi, the greatest footballer of all time, had a penalty. He can't score against Chelsea. He hits the bar. Chelsea go back to two lines and chase, and block and tackle and boot. We have 28% of the possession. Chelsea have stopped trying to play football and wait and see if Barcelona can break 6 years of Champions League injustice. They give everything and get nothing. Frank Lampard, in the final minute boots the ball up the Nou Camp's ridiculously long football pitch. Gary Neville: 'heee's in, heeee's in, ahhhhhhhhhhhhh' (Torres bobbles the ball past Valdez and puts it in the net) 'UNBURLEEEVERBALL'. Chelsea are through to a Champions League final in Munich, against - Bayern Munich.

Chelsea's starting XI against Bayern Munich was perhaps the weakest side we have ever fielded in any Champions League match with Boswinga at Right Back, Kalou in Midfield and Ryan Bertrand, normally a left back, making his Champions League debut on the left of midfield. Bayern Munich fielded players like Lahm, Kroos, Schweinsteger, Ribery, Muller, Robben and Gomez. If Chelsea were to win, we would need to defeat not one, but two of the greatest footballing sides assembled in the modern game.

I had been denied the opportunity to watch my team play because of my GCSE's and watched on from a friend's shed in Richmond surrounded by a QPR fan, two rugby fans and two Chelsea. We were completely outplayed. Muller scored a header in the last ten minutes and made a very annoying celebration. Even the most confident of Chelsea fans would not be criticised for losing confidence. Then, in the final minute, without one chance in 90 minutes, Didier Drogba scored from a corner. I am not a superstitious man. I don't believe it was written in the stars, and yet, there was something strange about the 2012 Chelsea squad. At the very moment you would write them off they would do something incredible. And then something stupid. And then something incredible. In the second half of extra time, Drogba gave away another penalty, then saved by Cech, taking Chelsea into extra time.

English football fans learn important lessons. Wear Adidas. Listen to The Clash. Beware of penalties – especially against the Germans who had defeated England at Italia 1990 and Euro 1996. Chelsea now faced Bayern Munich, a team that made up the majority of the German starting XI, in Munich. Lahm scored. Mata's first penalty was saved. Gomez scored. Luiz went top right. Neuer scored. Lampard went high and straight down the middle. Cech saved Olic. Ashley Cole curls the ball into the right corner hitting the side netting. Chelsea are level. Final two penalties. Schweinsteiger's saved from Cech. Drogba goes left, Neuer goes right. Chelsea are the Champions of Europe.

This was the perfect final for a relationship that had been the foundation of so much joy since the age of four. We had won the greatest prize in club football in the most extraordinary style. I was 16 and following my GCSE's would enter a new stage of life in which one specialises to offer something to our society in the same way the footballers do. I had learnt so much from the Chelsea side of Cech, Cole, Terry, Lampard and Drogba and in hindsight the Champions League final seemed like the end of an important stage in my life. I had imagined the world through football. Brazil, Argentina, The Ivory Coast, Ghana, Portugal,

Spain, Germany, Italy and France. I knew the footballing people of the world. Roberto Carlos, Ruud Gullit, Cesc Fabregas, Ray Wilkins. I had collected beautiful things. The sky blue Napoli Shirt, the teal Barcelona shirt. I had visited the world's greatest stadiums. Stamford Bridge, the Nou Camp and Wembley. I had seen goals that you would never have imagined. The Zola back flick from a corner against Norwich, Frank Lampard's free kick against Spurs in the Semi-Final of the FA Cup, John Terry's header against Barcelona in the Champions League Quarter Final. This was it. The amalgamation of all these fragments of memory synthesised into the greatest adventure in Chelsea history.

The Rugby Heineken Cup Final had taken place on the exact same day as the Champions League final. Rather fittingly, on the way home from the Chelsea victory, I got on a train with a company of Lenister Rugby fans who were celebrating European victory against Ulster. Amidst the Guinness and the singing, one Lenister man played the violin all the way back to Putney.

19th December 2021

THE BEATLES, ABBEY ROAD AND MY INTRODUCTION TO SUBCULTURE

Talking about Fellini and Dylan, Martin Scorsese wrote that 'they had touched legions of people, everyone felt like they *knew* them, like they *understood* them, and, often, like they *owned* them'. It is the nature of our deepest loves that we feel like they create and complete our greatest self. Through association with lyrics, sounds, styles or faces we use heroes to make a sense of who we are amidst the complex equation of consciousness. Culture is learnt. This transmission of knowledge has creative and intense diversions that make for excellent memories. In many situations, the conception of these relationships, the moment we first penetrate an idea, sets the tone and infatuation.

The first time I had the experience of love at first listen was at 6 years old finding *The Beatles 1,* a collection of all the Beatle's number ones, in my parent's CD collection. While I'm certain I had never listened to the Beatles there was an acknowledgement of who they were, likely as a result of watching The Simpsons or singing Yellow Submarine in Primary School. Like something from a 1960's girl's bedroom I took the album upstairs and started experimenting with the songs until I had a surge of energy through my body and started jumping up and down on my bed driven by Lennon and McCartney's piercing voice. The trigger was the 6th track on the album, *A Hard Day's Night.*

My family we're excellent enablers of my newfound love and played *The Beatles 1* on repeat through Swansea, the Welsh borderlands, Totnes and St Mawes. It was and will always be the soundtrack to spring and the soundtrack to summer. I learnt the lyrics. I learnt the harmonies. Then sometime later, I learnt the chords. It was on one of these trips that I met my greatest love, delivered in tape form from a Woolworths on the Welsh Borderlands and played in my Godmother's Peugeot. *Abbey Road* is simply the greatest album I have ever heard.

Abbey Road sequences and performs attitudes and emotions that I had never heard or felt anywhere else. It is a kaleidoscopic symphony of Hogarthian sketches, psychadelic harmonies and bluesy rock and roll. We are introduced to Mr Mustard, a girl who came through the bathroom window, an Octopus's Garden, a guy with no money after college, Polythene Pam and the Queen. Frank Sinatra, for many the voice of America and certainly the voice of Christmas, said that George Harrisons' *Something* was one the greatest love songs of all time.

One can feel the album's historical significance without knowing anything about the Beatles. It is communicated through the strength of songwriting, the confidence of subject and the experimentation with arrangement. Listening to *You Never Give Me Your Money* even a child can understand that something beautiful is dying, even a child can recognise that when Paul McCartney sings 'once there was a way to get back home' he is singing as much for himself as for the daughter. When we are told at the end of the album that the 'love you take is equal to the love you make' there is an intuitive sense that we are being given wisdom from a collective that has just years to live.

I learnt these lessons, these riddles, before I understood the power and influence of the Beatles. How is it, that there had been a planet over 40 years ago where people had experienced the exact same emotions – the same devotion – as I had. Five years after my first encounter with *The Beatles 1* the Arctic Monkeys released *Whatever People Say I Am, That's What I'm Not* and created the foundation for the subcultural infrastructure for most of my teens in Putney, Richmond, Chelsea, Wandsworth, Teddington and Kingston. And yet the centre of this lived experience remained in the past, with the stories and songs from the sixties. I listened to *Revolver, Sgt Peppers Lonely Hearts Club* and *The White Album* alongside *Favourite Worst Nightmare* and *Humbug*. The energy evoked is no less raw and the memories just as contemporary.

Loving the Beatles is a training in aesthetics, contrarianism, philosophy, sound, style, comedy, confidence, ambition, power and world domination. Through the Beatles I was given a fast-tracked education on Britain's cultural power in the 20th century. In a post-war order dominated by two superpowers, I expected my heroes to conquer America. I learnt through the Beatles, Queen, Pink Floyd, the Rolling Stones, David Bowie, Elton John, the Sex Pistols, the Clash, the Cure and Radiohead that America was Britain's for the taking. The transmission of song is very similar to the transmission of an idea. If you recognise from a very early age that a song, written in London or Liverpool, can impact the centre of an Empire you are gifted with a supreme sense of confidence about where you come from and where you are going.

In the century of the self, the Beatles provided characters that were perfect for the technology. On arrival to America on the 7th of February 1964 the Beatles' confidence was astounding. They are met with the full weight of communicative capitalism and simply smile, wave, sing and make jokes. These are four working class lads from Liverpool whose success would have been unthinkable just 20 years earlier. The attitude is phenomenal, and by no means anomalous. Of course, they had written some great songs, yet writing great songs doesn't correlate to being great teachers and cultural leaders - let alone beautiful, stylish and funny (imagine if we had had four Phil Spector's!). The Beatles were active participants in the most important aspects of 1960's Counter Culture. The Beatles gave the world psychedelic experimentation, meditation and the 20th century's greatest music. They were one of the West's greatest weapons in fighting the Cold War, with vinyl literally sold on the communist black market. They represented everything the USSR could never be. If you don't believe me then next time you are in Prague visit John Lennon wall, a country formerly under Soviet rule who dedicated an entire wall to a Liverpudlian musician that never visited the city. If you ever find yourself in Rishikesh make sure you visit the Beatles Ashram. Once the residence of the Beatles and the Beach Boys, this gutted counter cultural graveyard is covered in graffiti of Beatles lyrics demonstrating the Beatles contribution towards one of our most important Asian allies and the modern practice of Mindfulness.

China has just built a hypersonic missile that goes 16 times the speed of sound. We may not know how the Chinese built it, but I will confidently state that one day we will, and then also that China will never create anything more spontaneous, sexy and culturally challenging as the Beatles. In the context of the Cold War, they were our cultural nuclear weapon. They were James Bond, Don Draper, Charlie Chaplin and Picasso. They were a band of orators that created meaning to a world devastated by another famous orator who preached genocide and war instead of peace and love.

5th December 2021

BREATHING AND DRINKING –
CIGARETTES AND ALCOHOL

There is a South West train service that goes from Waterloo to Clapham Junction to Putney to Richmond to Teddington to Kingston and to Wimbledon. This route offers some of the most sought after space in Britain. Here we have the Oxford and Cambridge Boat Race in Putney, Roger Federer at Wimbledon Lawn Tennis Association and Johnny Wilkinson at Twickenham. I've described the area along the River Thames from Putney to Hampton Court as the Valley of Kings. This stretch of the river is defined by a series of 16th, 17th and 18th century palaces and houses. Starting at Fulham we have Bishops Palace, then Chiswick House, then Syon House, then Marble Hill House, then Ham House, under the steady watch of Pembroke Lodge built by John Soane and the former home of Prime Minister John Russell and the philosopher Bertrand Russell, then Orleans House and then Strawberry Hill House, finally, Hampton Court. Like the site surrounding the Acropolis rock, the neighbourhoods around the palaces and noble houses seem to be built in the style, image and perhaps even the same raw materials of these palaces and noble houses. The best example of this is the American University seen from the gardens of Ham House. Through activity, architecture and education, with the greatest schools in Britain located along this stretch of the Thames, The Valley of Kings is the realisation of the neo-classical dream.

Amidst this neo-classical symphony are kids, coming of age and experiencing life in the way that all kids do around the world. There are first loves and new experiences. Theatre, Debating, Literature, Science and Mathematics. Rugby, Football and Hockey. iPods and Smart Phones. Facebook, Gmail and SnapChat. Sex.

Cigarettes and Alcohol. It is the last two ingredients that formed the foundation for the engine of our social lives and the greatest connection between the people, the music and the films. Through cigarettes and alcohol, the teenagers raised on Britain's most holy fields transformed dark corners into a place of expression and freedom.

Breathing

A friend of mine had loved smoking so much that we spent one summer afternoon walking the streets of Putney searching for half smoked cigarettes. We collected a handful of quarter smoked cigarettes which the friend tried to smoke with kitchen roll. This was the day of my first ever cigarette. Later, an older female friend of his bought a twenty deck of king size Marlboroughs which we smoked sitting in an empty carpark just off the Upper Richmond Road. It was the introduction to an activity that would be defining for a huge number of years. I was the first person to have smoked in my year group. As time went on fellow peers would signal the desire to smoke or have experienced the same with primary school friends in the parks and gardens between Putney and Hampton Court. After a school trip to visit the battlefields of the Somme, cigarettes were acquired on mass, smuggled through the Channel tunnel and smoked a mile from Hampton Court.

Smoking is illegal for everyone under the age of 16. Of much more concern were people's parents seeing us smoking. Therefore, in pursuit of the cigarette, we managed to turn dark, gross and secretive places into sites of freedom. We smoked at a place we nicknamed 'DOD' because of the Danger of Death sign. We smoked at a place called 'bench', which was just a bench in the middle of a common. From summer to winter we smoked on the railway bridges and roads around the train lines from Clapham, to Putney, to Richmond, to Teddington, to Kingston, to Wimbledon.

In these spaces, we smoked cigarettes, blems, bloims, cigs, smokes, roll ups and straights. At first, we smoked 10 decks of Mayfair and Pall Mall, acquired through waiting for up to an hour outside of off-licenses. 10 decks were 3 pounds, 20 decks were 5 pounds. Then later when we had learnt to roll and obtained fake id's from siblings or travel shops that allowed the individual to offer a false age, we would smoke rolling tobacco, Drum and Golden Virgina and Cutters Choice, all sharing the experience of hiding the materials in the dark and secret places in our bedrooms. The revolution in smoking took place when Golden Virginia created a box of cigarettes that came equipped with five sticks of filters, rolling paper and 8 grams of Golden Virgina light.

The choice to smoke was a symbolic investment on the people that smoked, the conversation, the music and stories enjoyed when smoking. Smoking was a symbolic form of association with the rock and roll stars and the characters we had seen in the films. The poetics and attitude of smoking were created through the Arctic Monkeys and Oasis most explicitly through the songs *Cigarette Smoker Fiona* and *Cigarettes and Alcohol*, and then songs like Jehst's *High Plains Drifter*; 'I sit by the river, a packet of Rizla and a flask full of liquor' and Jamie T's *Sticks and Stones* 'I was a ten a day, how d'you say little shit, white lightning heightening all my courage quick wit'. We found shared affinity from the marijuana experiences described in Mac Miller's *Another Night* and the Souls of Mischief song *'93 Till Infinity*. Television series like Mad Men (Lucky Strikes) and the Pacific (Camels) affirmed the aesthetic beauty of smoking in the third person. Through smoking, we were experiencing the true nature of our films and records, which later I would learn were created on the Valley of Kings. Bob Marley and Led Zeppelin recorded between Chiswick House and Fulham Palace, The Rolling Stones performed near Ham House, The Beatles made records and Michael Caine made films just up from Marble Hill House and the films of Stanley Kubrick, George Lucas and Ridley Scott were created not far from Hampton Court. It's worth remembering that many dressed in the songs and clothes we had seen in *This Is England* wearing Fred Perry, Lyle and Scott and Adidas, some of us going beyond JD Sports and finding Merc and Baracuta on eBay.

Smoking was a motive in itself. The measurement of our excitement was very often articulated through Holidays in the Mediterranean. On family holidays in Nice and Sardinia, the sight and smell of Marlborough Lights, very often smoked by tanned French women, became my greatest object of desire. When the Ypres cigarette smugglers went to Malia and Sicily the freedom of the Trip was declared through the acquisition and smoking of cheap twenty decks. Through smoking, one pays great attention to the breath. In the Mediterranean, the alteration in temperature and proximity to the ocean is experienced through the inhalation and exhalation of the cigarette.

Drinking

The first experiments with alcohol felt of great significance. We were forming memories of serious consequences to our social bonds. On one night someone learnt the rules to Ring of Fire and the evening ended with the ecstasy of phones being smashed and a Ralph Lauren shirt disappearing from someone's body never to be found again. These dark nights of wit and mischief were the conversion to our new favourite game. Parents' cupboards were raided when staying over and sometimes looted at parties. We were at the behest of what our parents hadn't drank, in some cases, the parents hadn't drank for a number of years meaning that you had decades old Asda's basic vodka, blackberry liquor in ornate bottles and what seemed like a relentless supply of Disaronno.

In the game of cigarettes and alcohol, the off-license comes the paragon of excitement. It is where most of your money is spent on acquiring the two spiritual substances of tobacco and alcohol. The off-licenses themselves are a space of exoticism. They're normally run by a first-generation immigrant from South Asia. The stores are well stocked with cereal, washing powder, drinks, magazines, newspapers, sweets, chewing gum and sim cards, all designed with bright bold colours. Most off-licenses contain Ice Cream freezers despite the fact that we have few days in Britain where Ice

Cream seems necessary. Going to the off-license before a big night out is one of the rare times where your peers will entrust you with buying something on their behalf.

Beyond being funny, alcohol could solve problems and create opportunities. It gave one the confidence to talk in the way that one might like with strangers and the opposite sex and thus getting drunk became the winning method for expressing oneself and building connections after the age of 15. Alcohol is like a good coat. With a good coat, one has the ability to explore every area of a city in all temperatures. Similarly, after enough alcohol one has complete command over the social body and can access flow states of chain-smoking, flirtation and charisma. This is why drinking very often has the ability to stimulate some of the best and most honest conversations, with everyone able to express themselves with full social confidence.

The strength and reliability of alcohol to offer complete control of the body can lead to a dependence. If one feels like they can only have social control of the body after the aid of two pints they are in a very dangerous situation where socialising becomes conditional upon sufficient consumption of alcohol. This has the ability of creating the world of drinking and non-drinking. The world in which you are able to perform yourself with alcohol and the world in which you aren't. This rhythm of life can be intense and boring, spending five days in anticipation of drinking on the weekend. This relationship can feel pavlovian and leaves one's faculties of confidence weaker, enfeebling bodily strength. If I hadn't learnt how to meditate, I might still have believed that alcohol was the greatest way of dealing with the mind. Was I to have learnt to meditate at the same time as learning drinking I would have made much better decisions throughout my adulthood.

Like music, variations of alcohol created and drank vary depending on the geographical location. Korev in Cornwall, Guinness in Dublin, Draught Bier with huge frothy heads in Bavaria, Youngs at a Young's Pub, Fullers at a Fuller's pub, Beer

Peche when skiing in the Alps, Aperol Spritz on the Mediterranean and 600 ml bottles of warm Lion lager along the coast of Sri Lanka. In Putney, *The Rocket* was the meaning of life between 17 and 18. Other pubs worth mentioning include the Rayne's Park *Cavern* and *The Asparagus* in Clapham Junction. Regardless of location, the Arctic Monkeys, the Pogues and the Streets made the best drinking music.

4th of March 2022

ALEX TURNER: ROCK AND ROLL GREATNESS

I have spent the last 14 years with the Arctic Monkeys. The lessons I learnt from songs like *Bigger Boys and Stolen Sweethearts* are as true at twenty-four as they were when I was ten. At 15 I bought Suck it and See. The next day I lifted the line '*still breaking hearts with the efficiency that only youth can harness*' for my end of year English exam. In the Summer of 2014, they released two songs, *R U Mine* and *Do I Wanna Know*. I was on holiday with a group of lads in Malia. Every night, following four pints of Amstel we rolled through to the Indie Bar where they played, alongside copious amounts of Oasis' *Cigarettes and Alcohol*, these two songs on repeat. Then the day of my 18th Birthday the Arctic Monkeys played at Earls Court. Finally, I had the chance to lay eyes on the man who had been with me all my life. Every bloke in the audience unsuccessfully attempted to reinvent the sweaty short back and sides into an Alex Turner quiff. In the five years until I would next see the Arctic Monkeys, I had fallen in love with someone else. We broke up the night of seeing them at the O2 arena, in part inspired by Turner's tales of adventure and romance.

I have often mused on the roots of greatness. What made John Soane design the most beautiful buildings in London? Why was Christopher Hitchens' cultural mind distinguished from other essayists? My conclusion is that one must consume all the cultural symbols that have come before them and then have the ability to reinterpret, imitate and innovate. John Soane's house in Lincoln's Inn is the greatest example of this, displaying the vast collections of Roman imperial architecture that was then appropriated for designs on The Bank of England, Petersham Lodge, Dulwich Picture Gallery. Christopher Hitchens had all major writers,

Orwell, Woodhouse, Marx, Dickens, to memory and then applied them to debates on abortion and the existence of God. It is, in a sense, choosing to stand on the correct shoulders of the correct giants and then making the most of your height advantage. Alex Turner did for sub-culture what Hitchens did for essay writing and Soane did for architecture.

The day when the Arctic Monkey's *Whatever People Say I Am, That's What I'm Not* became the fastest selling debut album in British music history, Alex Turner had been 20 for just 17 days. Zane Lowe describes *Whatever People Say I Am I'm Not* as the British equivalent of Nas's *Illmatic*. The former combined youth with mastery of British subculture, mixing punk distortion and Strokes riffs with the aggression of Grime and Larkinesque observations on youth culture in Sheffield. This was the equivalent of the hat-trick scored by Wayne Rooney on his Champions League debut; the moment where people realised this bloke, barely an adult, has mastered something that hundreds of millions of people idolise.

Fitzgerald wrote that 'premature success gives one an almost mythical conception of destiny as opposed to will power – at its worse the Napoleonic delusion'. Rock and Roll graveyards are full of bands that fail with the sophomore albums, the most haunting being the Stone Roses' *Second Coming* which considerably damaged the reputation of the band who with the song's *I Wanna Be Adored*, *She Bangs the Drums*, *Waterfall*, *Don't Stop*, *Made of Stone*, *I am the Resurrection* and *This is the One* had written arguably the greatest debut Indie Rock and Roll debut album.

The Arctic Monkeys did not fuck about. 16 months after *Whatever People Say I Am, That's What I'm Not* they came back with the Matt Helders drum roll, the high pitched shredding riffs, break in the drums, BER BER BER BERBER BER BER, drums come back, BER BER BER BERBER BER BER x 3 (pause) 'BRYAN TOP MARKS FOR NOT TRYING'. *Brianstorm* punches with the left, then *Teddy Picker* goes for the knockout. On *Favourite Worst Nightmare,* Alex Turner has more wit, more women, more power, more mischief.

They were playing themselves at poker; for every *Riot Van* and *Fake Tales of San Fransisco* there was an *Only One Who Knows* and *Old Yellow Bricks*. The mythical conception of destiny was matched by a Napoleonic conquest: they sold 227 thousand copies on the first week becoming one of the youngest bands to headline Glastonbury.

Where does one go after conquering the world? Following the first two albums, Turner went from lippy British lad to confronting two of the most powerful archetypes in British culture in his project The Last Shadow Puppets where Turner and Miles Kane wrote the soundtrack for a mod James Bond, sporting Ben Sherman coats, riding on Soviet Tanks through Eastern European snow.

They say that you can judge a man by the company he keeps. Turner picked strong representatives of British subculture. He cited punk poet John Cooper Clarke as his 'hero', was an associate with Chris Morris later working with Richard Ayoade on the soundtrack for *Submarine*. Turner was learning the symbols and archetypes that had monopolised the British subcultural imaginations of Rock and Roll and film and then was reinterpreting and introducing them to a new generation on a much bigger stage. This was a frontman completely aware of what to write, say, wear and learn.

The Arctic Monkeys' third album *Humbug* marks the creative maturity of Turner. As described by Drummer Matt Helders, it is the transition from anti-rock stars to rock stars. They had left Sheffield, the Fred Perry polo shirts and the models for the challenge of defending the title of Rock and Roll star, previously held by John Lennon, Mick Jagger and David Bowie. At the age of 14, I was disappointed. They were about LSD, Josh Homme and the desert. I was beginning to drink, smoke and pull. The Arctic Monkeys had grown up whereas I was beginning to live the first two albums.

The combination of Humbug's heavy guitars with the laddy wit of the first two albums is best encapsulated through the *Suck it and See* B-Side *Evil Twin*. Turner snarls, bearing sharp teeth, over a steaming riff: *'you've never met before/ but still she greets you like a long lost rock and roll/ she's definitely one of those/ where you go wherever she goes'*. The greatness of Alex Turner's song writing has been defined by the bands B-sides, *Temptation Greets You Like Your Naughty Friend, Settle for a Draw, Cigarette Smoker Fiona, Anyways,* which are the rock and roll equivalent like playing the 2010 Spain team and seeing Fabregas, the Liverpool Torres, David Silva and Jesus Navas on the bench.

By the fourth album *Suck it and See*, a piece of graffiti found on the wall in Alex's apartment block in *Clockwork Orange*, Turner had stopped observing the prosaic and started to create their own eccentricity where black treacle and dandelion burdock sat alongside the band's toughest midfield outlet of *Don't Sit Down 'Cause I've Moved Your Chair, Library Pictures* and *All My Own Stunts*. Turner was in Holland Park surrounded by peacocks picking off marble goddesses with a shotgun.

The greatest collective moment for *Suck it and See* and the next album *AM* was the 2013 return to Glastonbury. When the Arctic Monkeys first played, they had been under experienced and scruffy. This time, Turner's Elvis haircut didn't have a strand out of place. The audience was under Turner's command with the lead singer slowly swaying the hips and casting out the hand like a Jedi using the force. The final song has Turner bring back Miles Kane for 505. Kane plays the guitar. Through cigarette smoke, Turner sings *'in my imagination you're waiting, lying on your side/ with your hands between your thighs'*. The streetwear and fringe have gone but he keeps the Sheffield accent. 'Glastonbury – Thank You Vary Moch'.

With AM, Turner loses the queer eccentricities and finds whisky soaked abstractions, telling tales of seeking and rejection over distorted doo wops. Turner's in Los Angeles on a conveyer belt of cocktail parties and love affairs. Leather jacket. Sunglasses indoors. *'suddenly it hit me it's a year ago/ since I drank miniature whiskey and we shared your Coke/ Said, ain't it just like you to kiss me and then hit the road?'*. I'm in sixth form screaming 'one for the road' getting Budweisers from off licences on Putney High Street before taking buses to Kingston for 18th's. *'so we all go back to yours and you sit and talk to me on the floor'*. With AM Turner offers the best pictures of a self deprecating over boozed and oversexed creative confidently asserting talent while fully aware of his faults. Turner ends the album with a cover of John Cooper Clarke's *I Wanna Be Yours*.

Then came the great pause. The Arctic Monkeys left us for 5 years – the time when life changed beyond belief. Brexit. Trump. Trauma. Destruction. Turner quits the Elvis persona adopting the style of Robert De Niro in the opening scenes of *Deer Hunter*. Globalisation's being rejected. Turner's been in isolation with a Steinway creating *Tranquility Base Hotel and Casino*, an American trip that combines the tackiness of Trump Tower and the Taj Mahal Casino with the interior designed by an acid soaked Hunter S Thompson. Jesus's in the Day Spa. Trump's walking around in golden wrestlers' underpants. The Arctic Monkeys play as a cover band in the bar that looks like one found in Star Wars *A New Hope*. These are the last days of the American Empire. Hendrix plays the national anthem to an emptied Woodstock littered with tablets and ponchos. The band missed the last helicopter out of Saigon – in truth they never even bothered to get on it. Now, Chandler from Friends, Peter Thiel, Buzz Aldrin, John Cena, Louis Farrakhan and Sarah Palin drink Cosmopolitans as Turner asks, 'Who remembers this one?'. The audience stops talking. Turner starts to sing *Cornerstone* the American exiles continue in hushed conversation. Western Liberalism's sweetest son, the rock and roll star, maybe the last of his kind, sings us out of hegemony:

*'just as the apocalypse finally gets prioritised
And you cried some of the hottest tears you ever cried
multiplied by five
I suppose the singer must die'*

It's the death of the 60's reimagined for Trump's America.

The boy wonder sporting baggy jeans and an Adidas zip up explained the idiosyncrasies of British life in the early 2000's better than a generation had thought of. Turner took us from a reality where *'there's only music so that there's new ringtones'* to *'the exotic sound of data storage'*. From the exuberance of millennial youth to the foyer of a decaying superpower. He went from Girls Aloud to John Cooper Clarke to Josh Homme to Richard Ayoade and Miles Kane. And now he sits on his own in isolation at the piano *'Perhaps it's time that you went for a walk/ And dress like a fictional character/ From a place they called America/ In the golden age.'*

17th of May 2020

POST DUBSTEP

There was a time when the iPod was my spirit animal. Every emotion would be regulated or matched with the sounds I found through Thursday nights on the desktop computer. I would search through the NME, Radio 1, Radio 1 Xtra playlists, Zane Lowe and then always to a blog called *post dubstep*.

Secondary School in London was very urban. Working class slang would be acquired and flexed to intimidate peers and demonstrate one's confidence in and connection to the city. Similarly, sounds and styles from subcultures would be played and worn as the defining feature of an individual's status.

Dubstep and Grime were introduced almost immediately after graduating from primary to secondary school. The appeal of this music was its ability to paint imagined futures and violent diversions from our present understanding of London. With Dubstep there was the ability to find yourself connected with the nightclubs, Fabric, Corsica Studios, Lightbox, which were out of our reach for the next 4 or 5 years. With Grime, Dizzee Rascal, Sway, Wiley, Skepta, JME, Giggs, we learned lessons about attitude, honour, sexuality, socialising, masculinity, respect and aggression. Nonetheless, the stories about the black experience in working class London were still far away from my own understanding of the city and thus, like how Dubstep was made for the clubs, Grime seemed somewhat removed from my day today experience.

We didn't have the gangs, the weapons or the clubs but we did have iPods, bus journeys, free yards and gatherings. Dubstep and Grime found a lived existence within the free yards and gatherings where the groups 'musical ones' would spend the evening crowded around a set of speakers flexing finds and trading tracks. And yet, beyond these celebratory spaces, the enjoyment of Dubstep didn't seem made for the iPod and the subjects of Grime seemed like a sport played within very specific theatres within the metropole.

Therefore, it was the sound that I will call *post dubstep*, artists like Jamie XX, Burial, Four Tet, Mount Kimbie, James Blake, Koreless and Mala, that soundtracked the geist of the city - its tubes, its train stations, its bridges, its bus stops, its darkness, its slickness, its lights, its people, its energy, its clubs.

Using the rhythm of Grime, the base of Dubstep, the soul of songs chopped and screwed from previous subcultures, *post dubstep* created music in bedrooms for Londoners to walk, commute or watch the city. Songs like Mala's *Alicia*, James Blake's edit of Drake's *Up All Night*, Four Tet's *Plastic People*, Burial's *Untrue*, Jamie XX's *Far Nearer* and Mount Kimbie's *Before I Move Off*, sound like they are tailor made for a modern urban landscape of 17th century cathedrals, brutalist architecture, buildings designed in Norman Foster studios and the endless stream of bright lights and big ideas.

17th of June 2021

IN DEFENCE OF NOISE: RAVE CULTURE AND THE NIGHT CLUB

I'm regularly asked about the best gigs I have been to. Whilst the Arctic Monkeys at Earls Court in 2014 and Radiohead at the Pyramid Stage in 2017 are two of the greatest moments of my life the fact is that my best live music experiences have been through the DJ and the Nightclub. In regard to subculture, the greatest difference between my parents' generation and mine is the arrival of rave culture. In the 90's through DJ's and nightclubs, an entirely new subcultural scene emerged with the creation of musical genres like Jungle, Drum and Base, Techno and Dub Step. The way that this music is enjoyed, loud and immersive from the hours of midnight to 6 am, was something new to our country. If you are young enough to have raved till sunrise then you have experienced one of the greatest joys of Western Liberal modernity. These experiences are the complete immersion and connection with sound and vibration, manipulating the mind into feeling good much longer than the body is used to.

To rave is to activate one of the most exhilarating constellations of the urban infrastructure. The corner shop, the Tesco's, the Pre's, the conversation and music at the pre's, the Taxi, the interaction with taxi drivers, the street lights, the roads, the human traffic, the bouncers, the nightclub, the different rooms, the crowd of people from different classes, ethnicities and sexualities, the eye contact, the inspection of the generally strange industrial space in the smokers, the sober barman, the food from the local kebab shop, the exhaustion. Aside from work, in going to a rave you are spending the longest time that you ever spend in the middle of a city. Normally, raves will last 8 hours, with people arriving at midnight and leaving at around 5 or 6 am. In London, you spend 6 hours in Smithfield's at Fabric. In Bristol, you are spending 6 hours on Stokes Croft at Lakota and in Manchester you spend 6 hours underneath Manchester Piccadilly at the Warehouse project. These evenings feel like 6-hour meditations on the soul of the city.

Attending the University of Bristol between 2014 and 2017, the city exhibited the greatest side of rave culture. Because of post-war West Indian migration, the city hosted a good deal of post-colonial spaces that formed the roots of modern Bristol's greatest subcultural exports. During the 60's Bristol had West Indian clubs like the Bamboo club hosting greats like Bob Marley, Desmond Dekker, Jimmy Cliff and Lee Dorsey. Just as my first introduction to the performance of Sound System culture was at the Notting Hill Carnival many Bristolians are introduced to Reggae records and Dub Plates through St. Paul's Carnival. Post-colonial spaces were established around the University of Bristol's Wills Library. Next door to modern day Taka Taka was Revolver Records one of the country's greatest record shops in the 80's and then left of Wills Library underneath the White Hart Pub was the site of the Dug-Out nightclub. Hip Hop, Reggae and Dub music would be bought from Revolver Records and then played on sound systems at the Dug Out allowing groups like Massive Attack to hone talents at DJ'ing and MC'ing. Today it is places like Lakota, Thekla, The Love Inn and of course Motion that are the descendants of this sound system tradition. At University, if you weren't working then you were likely to be found in one of these nightclubs.

Two of the most important strands of modern rave subculture are from West Indian music and the European continent. The roots of Modern British rave music like Grime, Dubstep, Drum and Base and Jungle lie in West Indian Dub and Reggae. This cross fertilisation of DJ'ing and MC'ing is best exemplified through songs like the Newham Generals song *Hard* and the Plastician and Skepta song *I See You*. London music collectives like HyperDub and Swamp 81 pay homage to their West Indian roots in the name of the label. The other strain of musical subgenres that dominate Britain's best nightclubs are European exports. The rave scene has created space to furnish European subcultural superstars, who through playing music without lyrics, or simply other people's songs, are able to transcend language barriers. Festival line-ups are a testament to a strength of cultural connection between English speaking peoples. Primarily Glastonbury hosts artists from Britain, Ireland, Canada, the USA and Australia. Performance wise, Glastonbury, a festival helped set up by Arabella Churchill, is the realisation of the cultural community of Winston Churchill's English Speaking Peoples. However, come nightfall, find yourself in Shangri-La or Bloc 9 and there is a huge chance that you will come across European superstars like Hunee, Antal, Amelia Lens, Ben Klock, Gerd Janson or Marcel Dettman playing disco, house and techno. Aside from Nico, Hans Zimmer and Kraftwerk, Techno is the only modern German export to have been established in Britain and sounds like music from the front line of the Cold War as demonstrated in the David Bowie album *Low.* Therefore, whilst Europe has been largely absent from British mainstream culture the nightclub created a space where the European might become King or Queen.

Modern DJ's are academics of sound. They have spent thousands of hours with records. They have to have heard everything that everyone has listened to and everything that no one has listened to. Playing sets, they have to specialise in multiple genres and excel at least one. When they are selecting sets, they have to respond to the emotion of the audience, the social context and the spatial and locational environment. A DJ set is like a collage or an algorithm. Every song compliments the next contributing to the whole. For artists like Four Tet and Ben UFO, they have to select other people's music that will bring the most from their own. The best DJs are obsessives that are keen to know more music and play it better than their peers.

The phenomenological experience as a raver is an extreme and intense immersion of the senses. Songs like Mike Skinner's *Blinded By The Lights* and Jamie XX's *All Raving Under One Roof* provide excellent descriptions of these symposiums. The nightclub smells like sweat, smoke machines, cigarette smoke and marijuana. The strobe lights are bright and constant. There is the taste of alcohol and energy drinks. There is a strong sense of physical intimacy, some romantic some uncomfortable. There are the acute variations in sound waves depending on where you are in the club. There is vibration through all the walls. There is the foundation of dancing in the two step followed by the swaying of the head, the extension of the arms and the pointing of the gun fingers. There is the direct link between your body and the sound waves reacting towards the arrival of every vibration on the eardrum. There is the rich form of bodily communication as people hug and dance. There is the consummation of flirtation. The amelioration of relationships. The staring into people's excited eyes. There is the awkward conversation in which you can't quite hear what someone says amidst the noise. There is the navigation to and from the smokers. There is the vodka mixer from someone's bag. There is the voice note recorded so you can find the song the DJ's playing. There is the release from virtual solitude, scanning thousands of pages of scholarly articles and books. There is the strongest display of the beauty and biopower of youth.

Through the nightclub, rave subculture has created palaces of noise and spaces that articulate and communicate the experience of Europe's urban centres and act as testaments towards the benevolent power of noise. These rare sites are built through the digital infrastructures of social media whose nature has been greatly experienced yet seldom conceptualised in the mainstream. In regard to the idea of post-war Britain, the nightclub has been one of the greatest spaces of cultural cross fertilisation.

16th of January 2022

LEONARD COHEN: THE HONEST PARTNER

As a teenager, the pursuit of finding new music seemed more concerned with the style and the social than with the literary. Cohen was an exception from most Rock and Roll stars. He attended Columbia University and prior to writing songs, was the author of two novels, *The Favourite Game* (1963) and *Beautiful Losers* (1966). This experienced command of the English language distinguishes Cohen from all other modern songwriters. It gives him the courage to confront themes of love, suffering and irony with an eloquence not expected from a guitar wielding performer.

When one listens to Cohen there is the immense sense that, through virtue of repeated plays, one may acquire the gifts of irresistibility to women and the command over an empire of emotions. The desire to become Cohen is based on more than just his songwriting. The songs act as a window to a polymath, a magician, a poet, a psychonaut, a man at home in Hampstead Heath, New York, Hydra, a member of one of the most powerful Jewish families in Montreal, a monk, a ladies man, a chain smoker, a novelist.

The gift of Cohen's songwriting stems from his honesty. Cohen is an artist who seeks to represent life as it is, articulating the truth merely for the power of doing so. The value of this quality is immense and the relevance of his words grow with all the slings and arrows of outrageous fortune.

Following the nomination of Donald Trump, it was the Cohen song *Everybody Knows* (1988) that provided the most effective insight towards the collective disturbance, singing:

'Everybody knows the war is over/ Everybody knows the good guys lost/ Everybody knows the boat is leaking/ Everybody knows that the

Captain lied/ Everybody got this broken feeling/ Like their father or their dog just died'

No other singer has articulated the fear of accelerating to a planet of 3 degrees of global warming better than Cohen in The Future (1992):

'Your servant here, he has been told/ To say it clear, to say it cold/ It's over, it ain't going any further/ And now the wheels of heaven stop/ You feel the devils riding crop/ Get ready for the future it is murder'

'Things are going to slide/ Slide in all directions/ Won't see nothing/ Nothing you can measure anymore/ The blizzard, the blizzard of the world/ Has passed the threshold/ And it has over turned the order of the soul'.

Cohen's lessons are free from the chains of ideology or retail. While Johnny Rotten may go from the Sex Pistols to advertising Country Life butter, Cohen is worthy listening from *Songs of Leonard Cohen* in 1969 until his last album, *You Want It Darker,* released just 17 days before his death on the 7th of November 2016.

So Long Marianne, found on *The Songs of Leonard Cohen*, introduces us to Leonard Cohen's longest love affair, conceived in Hydra and concluded on Marianne's death bed. *Songs from a Room* includes *The Partisan* a song originally sung by the French Resistance during World War Two and to my mind provides the best use of French in English popular music. *Famous Blue Raincoat* from *Songs of Love and Hate* provides a riddle of lost love and rivalry through the medium of a letter. *New Skin Old Ceremony* houses *Lover, Lover, Lover,* written during the time of performances to Israeli troops during the Yom Kippur War, the song is a vision of conflict through love, the self and the family.

Death of a Ladies Man, produced by a gun wielding and cranky Phil Spector, offers songs like *Memories* where Leonard Cohen injects 1950's ballads with a heavy dose of lust. *First We Take Manhattan* on *I'm Your Man* see's Cohen desire go from women to Empire.

Came So Far for Beauty on *Recent Songs* provides a story, familiar yet never articulated, of an individual who fails to gain respect for spiritual and aesthetic achievements. *Various Positions* provides Cohen's most famous song *Hallelujah* featured in The OC, The Watchmen and Shrek.

Ten New Songs provided the first Leonard Cohen album following a five year hiatus in the Mt. Baldy Zen Center. *In my Secret Life*, a song I first heard drinking in a beach hut in Gorkana, South India, Cohen confronts the difference between public persona of competition and conformity with the private persona of memory and principle. If you've ever thought what happens to lust around the age of 70, the song *Because Of* on *Dear Heather* provides an intimate expression of the carnal appetite. The song *Nevermind* on *Popular Problems* articulates political contradictions and resignation in the face of an objective understanding of the past; *'There's truth that lives/ And truth that dies/ I don't know which/ So nevermind'*.

On *You Want It Darker*, Cohen uses his final breaths to warn of the eternal struggle of existence. Cohen talks to the God of genocide, *'they're lining up the prisoners and the guards are taking aim'*, and the murderous middle class *'I didn't know I had permission to murder and to maim'*. In the last verse, Cohen sings the same words Abraham replied on the suspension of his son's sacrifice, *'hinenei hinenei/ hinenei hinenei'* (here I am here I am/ here I am here I am (Isaiah 6:8)) followed by *'I'm ready my Lord'*.

11th of June 2020

WORSHIPPING WOMEN: THE GREAT GATSBY AND THE ROMANTIC SELF

Every novel is a hypothesis. It is an accumulation and performance of ideas that may or may not hold true to ones own phenomenological reality. In some cases, they may hold thematic, metaphorical, observational or fantastical truths that make them valuable in absence of experiential data. The Great Gatsby has offered excellent guidance towards the phenomena of self that dominates the way many live life. The idea of self is that many of us live by identities and stories that we have created for ourselves and measure all of our successes, failures, joy and defeat, as a result of this story. In the case of Jay Gatsby, Daisy Buchanan is Gatsby's sense of self. The poetry and thought weaved around the image and memory of her are less to do with Daisy and more to do with Gatsby. Daisy is the image of aesthetic beauty, wealth, attitude and temperament that explain Gatsby's desire to achieve the American, or the New York, dream. She is a story which transcends the narrative of capital and power accumulation that has defined the individual Gatsby has become. Gatsby likes to offer the impression that Daisy, or his sense of Daisy, is the legitimation for the accumulation of wealth and power. Luhrman's film suggests that Gatsby's greatest desire is to associate himself with the symbols of old money or defeat the symbols of old money that have been denied to him through birth. This is demonstrated in Gatsby's pursuit of Daisy, where Gatsby's most violent reaction comes following the assertion from Buchanan that he was born different to himself and Daisy, suggesting that wealth anxiety is Gatsby's greatest source of pain. Therefore, Gatsby's sense of romantic self has been written around social, economic and psychological factors that allow him to make sense and meaning of his actions.

Fitzgerald writes 'no fire and freshness can challenge what a man can store in his ghostly heart'. Talking from experience, men have an extraordinary ability to dress women in symbols and poetry, making the romantic self one of the most potent parts that man can write for himself. Unfortunately, these desires are seldom egalitarian. In fact, a handful of women, perhaps even those that can be counted on one hand, have the ability to inspire and characterize a Gentleman's sense of romantic self. Fitzgerald says of Gatsby 'he knew that when he kissed this girl, and forever wed his unutterable visions to her perishable breath, his mind would never romp again like the mind of God'. When Gatsby replaces God with Daisy, he is replacing one faith for another. Like the Bible, Gatsby's idea of Daisy, the performance of a man that has spent thousands of dollars and hours conditioning his mind towards the image of Daisy, is an all encompassing narrative that characterizes his attention.

How is it then that a fictional narrative around the idealised person of the opposite sex can act as the single subject of someone's attention? Are men enfeebled or strengthened by an ability to be conditioned by a narrative sense of 'the one'? Are the chosen women aware of the power they possess within the minds of men? Are the chosen women aware of the symbolic power they possess within society?

What is certainly the case is that within situations where a woman becomes the measurement of a man's meaning and the expression of financial strength and imaginative creativity, that you have a recipe for mass instability and suffering. Men endowed with all their capabilities truly believe that a rare female is the true object of their investment and talent and hundreds, perhaps even thousands of men condition themselves - the books they read, the places they frequent, the clothes they wear - within the image of, say, five women. In addition, the more men invest themselves within these women the more they become associated with symbols and gifts that lead towards ever more swathes of men falling in love with these five women.

Of course, amongst these poetic narratives one may be able quite easily to point out similarities between the selected women, nonetheless, this doesn't take away from the fact that within the eyes of these legions of men, these femme fatales belong to them. Everyone creates a case, everyone writes a script, everyone belongs to a constellation of data points that evidence why they are the best suitor for the chosen femme regardless of whatever romantic situation these women may already find themselves in. Such is the competition surrounding these chosen women, the ability to win these woman's appreciation is a measurement of a man's greatness in relation to all the other men that desire her. The Great Gatsby allows us to experience the realisation of our romantic selves through violence, disappointment and stoical faith.

12th of December 2021

ALDOUS HUXLEY ON SYMBOLS, CONSCIOUSNESS AND THE BRITISH EDUCATION SYSTEM'S HIDDEN FLAWS

Two dystopian novels scaffold the collective imagination on the past, present and future. These are the worlds of totalitarian surveillance through *1984* and the scientific dopamine fuelled dictatorship in *Brave New World*. Following World War Two, Aldous Huxley, author of *Brave New World*, came to a series of conclusions about the meaning of human existence. *Island* tells the story of Will Farnaby's visit to the forbidden island of Pala. Farnaby is a mild mannered and polite journalist who is sent to persuade the Palenese people to provide access to oil assets on Pala. Huxley uses a Socratic dialogue between Farnaby and the residents of Pala to make sense of a philosophy concerned with meditation, yoga and community. For the weight and clarity of ideas discussed, *Island* deserves to be viewed with the same significance as *1984* and *Brave New World.*

Huxley criticises the British education system for failing to equip students with the ability to experience consciousness beyond symbolic learning. Farnaby complains that 'in the school that I went to we never got to know things, we only ever got to know words'. Huxley, one of the British education systems' greatest symbol manipulators, writes that humans cannot prevent their brains from creating symbols suggesting that the function of the symbolic mind is to 'turn the chaos of given experience into a set of manageable symbols'. While some of these symbols 'correspond fairly closely to some of the aspects of external reality... sometimes, on the contrary, the symbols have almost no connection with external reality'. Similar criticisms of the western understanding of how the mind functions are found in

Through the Doors of Perception. Huxley accuses the mind, evolved for biological survival, as being a 'measly trickle of the kind of consciousness which will help us to stay alive on this particular planet'.

In light of Palanese exercises in Yoga and Meditation, Farnaby realises he has not been equipped with the tools for contemplating consciousness. The most notable memory of contemplation comes through self-association with symbols, in his case the 'other world sensuality' of the changing light of the Porter's Gin advert seen from the window of his mistress's Charing Cross apartment. In antidote to Farnaby's desperate and confused attempts of deconstructing symbolic orders and experiencing consciousness, Pala offers mindfulness meditation, along with specific lessons on symbol manipulation. 'What we give the children is simultaneously a training in perceiving and imagining a training in applied physiology and psychology, a training in practical ethics and practical religion, a training in the proper use of language, a training in self knowledge'.

The benefits of awareness are described as providing a way of understanding consciousness through physiology and thus beyond symbolic thought. Meditation is said to enhance the individual's ability to read their physiology: 'the not you on the further side of consciousness will find it easier to make itself known to you on the side of physiology'. Awareness of consciousness is professed to enhance the experience of carrying out the most mundane and difficult activities: 'if you'd been shown how to do things with the minimum of strain and maximum of awareness, you'd even enjoy honest toil'.

Huxley, after a lifetime of being one of the British Empire's most prodigal minds provides a philosophy and argument for the nature of existence. Talking from the experience of graduating through a British education system virtually the same since Huxley's day, I will go out and bat for all the above assertions on symbolism, meditation, consciousness and the meaning of life.

How is it that despite being trained at London's best schools, the first and most significant expression of contemplation and thought came from the opening line of the K Koke song *My Deepest Thoughts* where the UK Hip Hop artist asserts 'I think I think too much'. Huxley's analysis of the failings of the British Education system are almost 60 years old, and yet have failed to be effectively translated and implemented.

It is time to stop the betrayal of our students. The most important lessons I have learned on symbols and consciousness are hidden from the British Education system. The British Education system and society must go through a 21st century enlightenment and attempt to provide millions with a sense of clarity and direction for the meaning of existence. If we fail to be taught about symbols, thought and consciousness we are limiting individuals from enjoying the complexity and strength of consciousness, enfeebling our brightest minds and inviting all citizens towards the unnecessary suffering caused by the highest degree of ignorance.

3rd of March 2021

SPACE, NETWORKS AND THE CHURCH OF ENGLAND

Phillip Larkin did not believe in God and yet a memorial has been laid in his name at Westminster Abbey. It might be argued that, through his 1954 poem church going, Larkin expressed the best articulation of the modern experience of Church of England Protestantism describing it to be:

'a shape less recognizable each week,
A purpose more obscure.'

My community in Putney is largely protestant. I attended the Church connected to my primary school until the age of 10. The majority of people I attended primary school with did not believe in God. Many of these people then attended Church of England secondary schools and still their faith did not surface. Following the graduation from primary to secondary school many parents left the church knowing, as Larkin did 66 years ago, that the church's goal of instructions on Christianity don't provide the necessary emotional, spiritual and intellectual guidance to navigate the modern world.

Phillip Larkin recognised something that still has not been remedied:

'wondering too,
When churches will fall completely out of use
What we shall turn into, if we shall keep
A few cathedrals on show,
Their parchment, plate and pryx in locked cases,
And let the rest rent free to rain and sheep. Shall we avoid them as
unlucky places?'

There are over 16,000 Church of England churches. Often these are the grandest and most central buildings in British cities, towns and villages. As implied by Larkin some 66 years ago, their spatial significance cannot be matched by spiritual impotence. The fact Larkin could be so critical about the function of churches and still be glorified in the site where they coronate the head of the Church, reads as an admission that the Church of England shares his judgements.

The disconnection between church and society is not as novel as Larkin's poem suggests. The deficiency of wellbeing within our networks and communities is most acutely exemplified at the moment when individuals graduate from the conventional structure of family and secondary school. The Guardian suggests there is a 'mental health crisis' at Universities. Between 2016 and 2019 there were 13 suicides at the University of Bristol. When terrible things happen, the University gets blamed and then responds by investing millions in mental health services, yet, clearly this 'crises' points towards a society where we are not teaching our children the skills to understand their minds and bodies and thus there is an impoverished sense of meaning. These are exactly the functions that a Church should play. In absence of these lessons, students grope for mental balance that will enable effective social functioning, generally manifesting themselves in drugs and alcohol. This cycle is vicious because the medicine is very addictive. The most addictive substance of all is social media and these platforms are, for the first time, the main site for governance and organisation, but also a crucible of gossip, communication and presentation. These three factors, limited knowledge of mental wellbeing, the search for connection and control through drugs and alcohol and the organizational importance of networked communications are the zero day vulnerabilities of British network building that are only realised at the moment of departure from the family and secondary school networks. When people describe identity politics as a new religion, this may encapsulate student desires to find meaning within themselves, and to be able to assert a faith in authority of identity over any confrontation with rational criticism. I believe that all these problems can be effectively treated by the transformation of the Church of England into a network and space that specialises in secular ceremonies and practices.

The importance of the Church of England lies in the significance of space within British communities. First, this can be established by confronting and undermining the views of Christopher Hitchens. Secondly by asserting that space, not Protestantism, provides the single most significant factor for the church and thirdly proposing content for the secular assembly.

Christopher Hitchens got it wrong when he asserted that 'there is no need for us (non-believers) to gather... every seven days or on any highly auspicious day, to proclaim our rectitude or to grovel or wallow in our unworthiness'. Hitchens provides an alternative sustenance of meaning through 'a leisurely or urgent walk from one side of the library or the gallery to another, or to lunch with an agreeable friend, in pursuit of truth or beauty'. This rejection of collective communion contradicts the actions of a man who spent a large amount of his time doing public speaking or debating at ticketed events to like-minded audiences. Unlike the Hitchens events, any meeting of non-believers within churches would be free. The orator may not have the ability of Hitchens, but the topics may well be similar. What Hitchens does not mention is the importance of church space in the creation of strong and healthy networks.

In the Putney of my youth church created the structure where you were effectively bought up by 4 or 5 parents (as suggested in Aldous Huxley's The Island) through virtue of regular connection and subsequent meetings within the community. The networks were built through the protestant spaces of school and church and then successfully migrated to secondary school. There were strong ties on the 85 bus route from Putney to Kingston through church, school, and scouts. The Church was very effective at network building, however, because these networks were grown through a space that lost relevance after the children graduated from primary school, children of 11 were divorced from a central space of network building. Surely it would be more effective to utilise the space of the Church into a communion of people that come together for a set of principles and activities that have relevance throughout people's lives. This means that the network successfully built for secondary schools would be sustained beyond the age of 10.

St.Mary's Church Putney

The importance of church lies in its spatial significance within the community connected to schools, providing a proximity towards friends and a space where people can contribute their time, effort and attention. These spaces are egalitarian and provide the ability to transcend race and class boundaries. Churches are built as oratorical spaces of collective communication. In Britain, protestant sites provide connection towards an area's history. During lockdown I found myself continually drawn toward the Putney graveyard because it displays a set of symbols, be they crosses or family names ('Musk, Hitchings, Wiggins') that provide me with a sense of connection towards the landscapes history. These places are characterised by the symbols of Protestantism but cannot be monopolised by the Church of England, yet are left bastardised by a space that no longer offers meaningful teachings. These spaces connection with landscapes may be characterised by Protestantism but cannot be monopolised by the Church of England as they exist and belong beyond faith. The spatial significance of protestant sites needs to be repurposed to enrich the families, partners and individuals that choose to reside in these areas.

The gifts of humanism, mindfulness and the counterculture provide rich lessons that could be taught at assemblies. The marriage of humanism and protestant space is best exemplified through Westminster Abbey were 'over 100 poets and writers are buried or have memorials' these include William Shakespeare, Jane Austen, the Bronte sisters, Geoffrey Chaucer, WH Auden, Dylan Thomas, William Wordsworth, Charles Dickens and of course Phillip Larkin. Christopher Hitchens calls upon these writers to navigate the non-believers 'sense of wonder and mystery and awe' writing '(we) find that serious ethical dilemmas are better handled by Shakespeare Tolstoy and Schiller and Dostoevsky and George Elliot than in the mythical morality role of the holy books'. A space that provided insight and introduction to such thinkers would provide evergreen enlightenment for all those that attended. These ideas and writers that mastered and played with the English language could be provided not by vicars but by guides. Beyond poetry and literature, the assembly could provide mindfulness lessons – the most practical way of recognising consciousness – walking, history, philosophy, science, climate change and nature. Like the church seminar the guide could give continual reflections about happenings within the local, national and international communities providing experience of in person articulation and dialogue that most find only at the theatre after paying £220 pounds. These assemblies, nights, seminars, whatever you call them, would replenish the collective intellectual and spiritual drought created by irrelevant politicians and the divorce from activities that once took place in protestant spaces.

Therefore, it is time to transform Church of England spaces in order to provide a secular service that will give communities the guidance they so need. There are over 16,000 Church of England churches who have not effectively served communities for a very long time. Nonetheless, these buildings are positioned in the most spatially significant areas for the community. The University mental health crises point towards an emergency in mental wellbeing that can be remedied by the creation of a rigorous infrastructure of spirituality that makes sense in the modern world. Community networks need to be built and sustained not until the graduation from primary school but throughout one's brief existence and assembly over shared principles, ideas and goals may well be one of the strongest and most egalitarian ways of providing this, meaning the Church of England offers the perfect structure for the reseeding of community ties.

25th of July 2020

SPACE, POWER, MEDITATION AND INTERNET TECHNOLOGIES

Power relations are played out in every space that one inhabits. A great deal of strategic thought and symbolism is enshrined within the spaces where we spend our time. Two of the most obvious relationships of power found through space are the body politic and wealth.

Certain capabilities may be expected to perform conventionally in a certain space, this therefore may be seen as a good example of the body politic. For one to be on stage in front of an audience they need to be able to act, for one to be on the football pitch it is expected that they play football, for one to be on the roads it is expected that they drive and for one to be on the ski slopes it is expected that they ski. All of these are measurements of capability that reflect an individual's bodily strength thus determining their position within given spaces. Special spaces are allocated to all that may have difficulty occupying the same space through disabled spaces, be it for a concert, cinema viewing or car park. Therefore, within public and private spaces there are power relations at play that are demonstrative of the biopolitics of capability and the spaces that people can inhabit are demonstrative of their capability in society. The ability to be capable enough to interact comfortably with space has a heroic element to it with individuals like Ernest Hemmingway and Christopher Hitchens performing strength through their capacity to inhabit and report on strange and often dangerous spaces. Historically racial discrimination has emphasised the most brutal differences in the body politic, with power being determined through the allocation of space in totalitarian regimes like Nazi Germany, Apartheid South Africa and the American South.

A lot of spaces are defined in part by capital. Normally, the spaces that people inhabit are private or belong to the state. Space has an inherent monetary value that is representative of the wealth of the given area. For instance, if a space is in a wealthy neighbourhood it is likely that that space will cost a lot of money. Therefore, individuals are likely to have access to similar spaces through virtue of their own wealth. The individual might socialise in spaces that are in themselves expensive and thus the friends that they make through these spaces are likely to be of a similar wealth to the host who has invited them, more explicitly, it is unlikely that people will visit a restaurant that they cannot afford. Therefore, the majority of spaces are determined or conditioned through, whether we know it or not, relations of capital.

Very often space can demonstrate a connective quality. A certain space is likely to give an indication of a social function. For instance, the experience of music, the experience of cinema, the experience of food, the experience of having the same memory, the experience of having the same DNA, in the example of church and the local pub there might be the collective experience of living in the same area. These qualities are central towards the creation of cultures and the building of networks. For instance, despite the ideas in Christianity being philosophically dull, the ability for the church to build strong social networks is great.

The practice of meditation and exploration of consciousness is conditioned and in part determined by the power relations at play within a given space. If meditation is the exploration of the senses – touch, taste, smell, temperature, pressure, sound – then the condition of these sensory experiences are determined through the contents of space. The food that you eat, the drink that you drink, the smoke that you smoke, the wi-fi that you use, the props, the tables, the chairs the cutlery, the oils, the steam, the tools are all determined by what one finds within space and the way space is conditioned is determined through conditions of biopower and capital. Meditation therefore might give one the means to understand conscious states that arise within certain spaces, but they are not able to prevent spaces' influence on consciousness. What's more, the space of consciousness has parameters. There are things that won't get heard. Sights that won't be seen through virtue of the parameter of sights within a room. There are sound waves that won't penetrate a certain space. There are smells that will not travel beyond certain rooms just as we have tastes that are only really experienced in the mouth. Given the influence of space on the states of consciousness it is important that meditation takes place within settings that are not likely to be threatening to the body politic. Of course, the study of meditation is about experiencing pain, but some kind of distinction needs to be made between the reflection of pain and the creation of spatial settings that will actively harm the body, even if the practice of meditation might make the harm manageable and interesting.

It may be the case that Internet of Things devices' effect on space is one of the most effective lenses to measure the social impact of mobile phones and Laptops. Through smartphones and Laptops every space, public and private, has become a supernode. Within almost every space we have 4G mobile network connection, and or Wi-Fi, meaning that a 10 cm by 6 cm object transforms every space into an accessible area to the world's information and billions of other nodes. Generally, it is the case with the internet that everybody has access to the same spaces. Access towards these spaces is a result of widespread surveillance that allows the technology monopolies to accumulate data that can be monetized through schemes like targeted advertising. Therefore just as the internet has turned every space into an opportunity to connect and assimilate knowledge, it also served to implement an oppressive form of biopower through virtue of knowing that you are unable to achieve privacy in the presence of an internet enabled device that may either be in the physical space or outside of it, through belonging to someone within the physical space or someone that is connected towards the individual within the physical space moreover, all spaces now tend to have a series of surveillance devices within them as people always carry a smartphone. This will serve to influence the capabilities needed to effectively inhabit and perform within a given space, an example being the workers' ability to be monitored digitally instead of physically. The ability to raise capital within narrow spaces is a result of the power of Internet of Things devices. This has been exemplified through the Coronavirus where businesses managed to function effectively in absence of a collective space through the capability of the internet.

The performance, occupation and connection of space offer detailed insight to how power functions. In many ways the biopower and character of an individual can be determined through the spaces that they inhabit. Relations of capital are greatly emphasised through private property but also the individuals that coalesce within that private property. The practice of meditation, despite offering the ability to connect with the senses, cannot be removed from the trappings of space, biopower, capital and technology, although it may well strengthen one's biopower capacity and will certainly give them a more accurate understanding of the quality of space that will likely lead to more insightful observations on power relations. Space has been completely transformed through virtue of the mobile phone as every space becomes a connection to all other nodes of society in a variety of creative and complex ways. In turn, the power relations associated with carrying a mobile phone add another complex layer towards the impact on space and the accessibility towards digital spaces within small physical spaces.

28th of July 2021

THE CRISIS IN DIGITAL COERCIVE CONTROL

Demos' November cybercrime report titled *The Great Surrender* provides a short and powerful statement: 'one thing is certain we are under attack'. *The Great Surrender* paints a picture of Britain and America in crisis as order and society is being dismantled by the infrastructure of the internet led 4th industrial revolution.

The true scale of cybercrime is unknown. Demos found that 70% of victims never reported the crime. Previously the City of London has given the figure of 80% of unreported cybercrimes. Of those that do report cybercrime, dissatisfaction is great. 50% expressed disappointment with Action Fraud, the UK's National Fraud and Cyber Crime Report Centre. Moreover, of the inadequate number of cybercrimes that have been reported, very few result in arrests. In the United States, less than 1% resulted in convictions.

The qualitative and quantitative data on digital coercive control provides the rawest articulations of how technology is increasing violence within society. ONS data from 2019 to 2020 showed there was a 110% increase in stalking cases, of which Paladin, the national stalking advocacy group, says most involve a cyber element. This makes stalking the most significant new crime in the United Kingdom. Cumulatively the ITV Tonight programme has recorded an increase of 1800% in cyberstalking cases from 2014 to 2018.

A five-year national survey in Australia emphasised the increase of digital coercive control through the National Survey of Technology Abuse and Domestic Violence. Some of the uses of cyberstalking are novel and chilling. There has been a 244.8% increase in respondents seeing perpetrators use GPS for the tracking of victim survivors. Partners have been targeted through their offspring, with a '346.6% increase in children being given phones to contact and control their mothers' and a '254.2% increase in the use of children's social media accounts by perpetrators' to contact guardians. These numbers read like a society where social bonds are dissolving through the utilisation, weaponization and deployment of technology. A UK investigation into digital coercive control, similar to the WESNET survey, is greatly needed.

One of the most valuable pieces of data from the Australian National Survey investigation was a comment from a domestic abuse practitioner explaining how the impact of digital coercive control was: 'unmeasurable. More than anything else, like rape, torture etc. That I've seen over the years, abuse with technology is so invasive and psychologically destabilising'. This comment makes it clear that we are witnessing a societal mutation different to previous forms of violence and domestic abuse. Another respondent emphasised that the police were failing to conceptualise this new beast, writing that 'high levels of coercion and control are actually the best indicator of risk to the victim rather than physical violence'. The qualitative data suggests that society has failed to effectively conceptualise the risk of digital cyberstalking and harassment, generally relying on heuristic tools and behaviours from a pre-internet age.

Andy Clark and Steve Chalmers develop the idea that the importance of internet of things devices is so much so that they are an extension of our minds. The ethical consequences of this would mean destroying someone's technology would be 'as damaging and reprehensible as a bodily attack', thus legally cyberstalking, stalkerware or hacking crimes could be interpreted as a form of physical assault. The violence of cyberstalking tools like stalkerware should not be underestimated, with one charity specialist suggesting that because of the anonymity provided and the capacity for violence, the introduction of these tools was worse than the introduction of guns into British society.

The accounts from the domestic cases may be symptomatic of an economy where surveillance is employed, even encouraged, in the workplace. The American Management Association suggests that at least 66% of US companies monitor their employees' Internet use, 45% log keystrokes and 43% track employees' emails. Britain's largest federation of trade unions, the TUC, has warned that 'staff surveillance is at risk of "spinning out of control"' and that 'about 60% of employed reported being subject to some form of technological surveillance and monitoring at their current or most recent job' and '3 in 10 respondents agreed that monitoring and surveillance at work had increased during the Covid-19 crisis'. Outside the context of income, the deployment of these methods emphasises the true face of digital coercive control.

You would think that if the means of securing law and order faced such grave threat, we would be mobilizing our civic, state and media apparatus towards effectively solving these problems. With relative silence from the press, a government that seems conscious of the problem but uninterested in action and a charity sector who are left burdened with providing the support the police can't, it is accurate to describe digital coercive control as one of the great modern threats to living lives of qualitative value.

Stephen Pinker's book *Angels of Our Better Nature: A History of Violence* argues that Hobbes' view of violence is an effective theory consistent throughout violence's history. Hobbes argues a state monopoly on violence is vital to prevent anarchical violence within society. Hobbes provides three reasons for anarchical violence: violence is used first in competition, with and over their wives, children and property. Secondly, to defend themselves and thirdly for reputation. With an impotent parliament, an uninterested 4th estate, and the absence of an effective police force, the internet infrastructure has overwhelmed traditional institutions and created conditions for violent anarchy. State, media and civil society should act with the greatest urgency, for right now it is the charities, The Suzy Lamplugh Trust, the Cyber Helpline, Women's Aid and Action Against Stalking providing the greatest insight towards the 4th Industrial Revolution's grossest products. If society cannot solve basic functions of law and order, then our governance systems and democracy will be called into question.

Demos are defending this gap in governance providing effective solutions for dealing with the cybercrime crises, my favourite being the establishment of a National Reporting Hotline for fraud and cybercrime with a simple three digit number providing the example of '119 for Cybercrime'. This would serve the function of a) showing that victims' experiences of cybercrime matter to the government and to law enforcement and b) removing much of the confusion around the reporting, which prevents victims from seeking help.

The need to reform the police is great. Steve Kavanagh, Britain's highest ranking British policeman, describes how 'this is the most profound shift the police have experienced since [Sir Robert] Peel [the Conservative statesman considered the father of modern policing]. We will adapt in a way more fundamental than anything since Peel's reform'.

In conversations that I have had with specialists, there has been emphasis on the need for disruptive police measures to create a sense of deterrent. I have previously written about the need for a cyber specialist police force in every geographical location in the United Kingdom.

According to Pinker the 'decline of violence may be the most significant and least appreciated development in the history of our species' and therefore the emergence of tools that threaten peaceful society should be addressed very seriously.

December 17th 2020

SNAPCHAT MAPS AND THE INFURIATING IDIOCY OF THE SURVEILLANCE ECONOMY

There are some things in the Surveillance Economy that are so explicitly ignorant that it defies ethical sensibility. On a planet where there are so many narcissists priding themselves on being smarter than everyone else how is it that we have so much passivity and ignorance on things that violate the moral standards of individual freedom? In the face of simple standards of principle, the intelligent narcissist gets exposed as a coward.

The most horrifying tool that I have seen on social media is the introduction of Snapchat Maps. Snapchat Maps takes surveillance to the next level allowing Snapchat users the ability to permanently share their geolocation with fellow Snapchat friends'. This feature is terrifying for the following reasons:

First, social pressure means that children are being coerced into permanently offering their geolocation to fellow SnapChat 'friends'. According to the LSE, 23% of Snapchat users haven't graduated from high school, implying that there is a social expectation that high school users use Snap Maps as the foundation for online social interaction.

Second, children are likely unaware of the risks associated with cyberstalking and online harassment. Cyberstalking has become the most significant new crime in Britain. Between April 2020 and March 2021 stalking cases increased from 32,000 to 98,863 between April 2020 and March 2021 making it the UK's most significant new crime. Paladin, the national stalking advocacy group, says most stalking involves a cyber element. Moreover, 13 to 18-year-olds are politically powerless, they cannot vote and thus are theoretically voiceless in regard to communicating their attitudes towards the adoption of social media tools. This lack of communication between social media users, adults, politicians and technology companies are likely an explanation for why lawmakers and the media focus greatly on subjects like self-harm and suicide because these actions are the only time that children are able to make contact with social media companies. This demonstrates a failure in communication between young people and the social media companies that is likely to lead to a product focused on the extraction of behavioural data and a deadly disregard for the user.

Third, Snapchat is normalising unprecedented levels of social surveillance at a very early age. From the point of view of Snapchat Maps, this is excellent because it gives them access to geolocation data which is a very lucrative form of behavioural data. In regard to the Snapchat users, they are being conditioned and indoctrinated to adopt morally contentious behaviours without the ability to formulate opinions on surveillance or mount an effective political response. Moreover, Social Media companies provide very little medium for the user to make complaints.

Fourth, Snapchat friends are very often casual and loose ties that one may have met once or twice at a party or social gathering. While it is acceptable to become social media 'friends' with someone after meeting just once, it is completely unacceptable that after meeting someone once they are then provided your geolocation data for the rest of your life spent on Snapchat.

Social Media tools condition modes of behaviour. Snapchat invites people to send second long flash images, Instagram invites people to upload pictures to a blog and Whatsapp invites people to send messages. Such is the fundamental drive for sociability amongst primates, if the social media site which is used by billions invites people to use a tool, they are creating social norms and thus through Snap Maps unreasonably coercing them into a form of behaviour that compromises the limits of individual consent. This exposes the gross social reality being implemented by Snapchat, where it would be 'anti-social' to attempt to protect oneself from 'abduction, physical and mental abuse, sexual abuse and trafficking'.

7th of October 2021

9 INSIGHTS FROM WORKING
WITH EXTINCTION REBELLION

From the 23rd of August to the 4th of September 2021 I conducted Media Monitoring for the Extinction Rebellion media team, analysing every article about XR during the protest. Having conducted similar work on behalf of XR for the 2019 international rebellion, I am probably one of the best positioned people on the planet to emphasise the merits, successes and criticisms of the world's most effective climate protest infrastructure. Below I have provided the 9 key insights from analysing the 2021 rebellion.

1. Every article that criticised Extinction Rebellion failed to mention the Paris Goals and the IPCC report.

2. With 650 groups in 45 countries, XR has become the greatest global infrastructure for the participation in climate protest.

3. XR's most effective when representing the global climate struggle and represents those that cannot stage internationally significant protests or may not be able to protest at all because of political repression. XR exhibited this political and moral leadership through actions outside the Brazilian Embassy against the destruction of the Amazon Rainforest and the destruction of indigenous communities.

4. The media and social media coverage of XR events in London make it representative of the global climate crisis. Media outlets like the Guardian, the BBC, and the Times are enjoyed globally and news on Social Media sites like Instagram, Twitter and Facebook is communicated to all countries.

5. XR seem scared of engaging with the question of China which is understandable given Chinese aggression towards criticism. Nonetheless, we cannot ignore the question of China's use of fossil fuels. 85% of China's energy comes from fossil fuels. 60% from coal. It has been reported that China is adding 'three new highly efficient coal mines each month' and a 2019 Greenpeace East Asia study indicates that China has put over five times more coal power into the Belt and Road Initiative than into wind and solar, moreover, through the Belt and Road initiative 'China's commercial banks face few restrictions on funding coal fired plants', with coal plants being built in European sites like Bosnia and Herzegovina.

6. Extinction Rebellion did a very good job of associating themselves with the IPCC science. While we have political representatives working in response to the IPCC Science, Extinction Rebellion are the most significant participatory expression of the climate anxiety and communication of the 6th IPCC report.

7. The climate struggle is essentially a strategy game. If you have the ability to understand these four points, then you can understand and communicate the climate struggle:

i. The idea that humans are responsible for the climate crises as a consequence of burning carbon.

ii. The IPCC predictions of the rate of global warming – the latest report suggests that 'we are now expected to release enough carbon emissions to cause the planet to warm by 1.5 C by 2040, although with the current trajectory of emissions this will likely be closer to 2034'.

iii. The international climate goals signed by 197 countries pledging to stay below 2 C by the end of the century and preferably to 1.5 C.

iv. The predictions of what happens at every stage of warming. For instance:

'*at two degrees, the ice sheets will begin their collapse, 400 million more people will suffer from water scarcity, major cities in the equatorial band of the planet will become unliveable, and even in the northern latitudes heat waves will kill thousands each summer. At three degrees, southern Europe would be in permanent drought, and the average drought in Central America would last 19 months longer and in the Carribean twenty one months longer. In northern Africa, the figure is sixty months longer – five years. The areas burned each year by wildfires would double in the Mediterranean and sextuple, or more, in the United States. At four degrees, there would be eight million more cases of dengue fever each year in Latin America alone and close to annual global food crises... Damages from river flooding would grow thirtyfold in Bangladesh, twentyfold in India, and as much as sixtyfold in the United Kingdom... Conflict and war could double*' (David Wallace Wells, the Uninhabitable Earth)

If you can understand these four points, then you are able to understand and communicate the climate struggle.

8. The electoral significance of Extinction Rebellion's Impossible Rebellion: The most significant evidence of XR's influence on politicians is to be found through the Guardian reporting how, at the same time XR protests were to begin around the London Stock Exchange, the Liberal Democrats introduced a policy that 'new listings of fossil fuel companies would be immediately banned on the London Stock Exchange' and 'Fossil fuel firms already listed in the UK would then have two years to produce a coherent plan about how they would reach net zero emissions by 2045, or risk being struck off the LSE'. 2 days after XR protested on London Bridge to 'make pensions green', the Liberal Democrats introduced policies to 'disinvest from fossil fuels by 2035, with all companies with fossil fuel assets removed from the exchange by 2045'. Zeynep Tufekci emphasises that the success of 21st-

century hyper-networked movements lies in the ability to affect narrative capacity, disruptive capacity and electoral capacity. Through the Impossible Rebellion, XR have effectively exhibited strong narrative and disruptive capacity. The Liberal Democrat's policy pledges strongly align with the action of XR protestors demonstrating significant evidence of XR's electoral impact on politicians.

9. Extinction Rebellion has a unique ability to hold private companies accountable through civil protest: three days after Extinction Rebellion demonstrated outside the Science Museum in response to an exhibition which had received Shell's sponsorship, the FT reported Shell's offer to install 1/3 of Britain's on street electric charging sites. XR hasn't been mentioned in the article, yet given this report came just three days after the protest, the correlation suggests it is a direct response from Shell. Beyond company policy, unlike critical journalists, Shell were keen to respond to XR protests with climate science stating that 'we seek to avoid, reduce and only then mitigate any remaining emissions. Developing carbon capture and storage and using natural sinks are two of a range of ways of decarbonising energy'. Companies are aware that they are guilty. XR protests will make them terrified fearing that they may lead to mass civilian international protest and boycott. XR's actions holding one firm accountable may serve as representative to all fossil fuel companies.

11th of December 2021

CAN CHINA SAVE THE WORLD
FROM CLIMATE DISASTER?

China has been the world's largest energy consumer since 2009, accounting for 25% of the world's energy consumption. China is responsible for 25% of global greenhouse emissions. 85% of its total energy comes from fossil fuels. 60% of its total energy comes from coal. Moreover, through China's Belt and Road policy, the country has 'positioned itself as a major provider, in some cases the major provider, of the infrastructure of industry, energy, and transportation in much of the rest of the developing world' therefore, China's policy towards building the Belt and Road Initiative have great consequences for the carbon neutrality targets of all 131 countries involved in the scheme. As emphasised by David Wallace Wells 'on the matter of climate change China does hold nearly all the cards'. Only recently, China argued 'that it was entitled to burn fossil fuels just like developed countries that have benefited most from such practices', thankfully, the world's largest polluter has committed towards changing course, and in 2020 Xi Jinping pledged to stop carbon emissions before 2030 and to achieve carbon neutrality by 2060.

Two recent books on the energy industry evaluate China's effectiveness in enacting climate change reform. First, David Yengin's book *The New Map* emphasises the global context of energy crises. Secondly, the book *Green China* introduces empirical evidence for and against climate change mitigation efforts. Just as Christianity was the moral rhetoric supporting the British Empire and Democracy for the Americans, Shapiro and Yi suggest environmentalism is the civilising mission created to justify CCP authoritarian imperialism.

China has the greatest technological capacity to build renewable energy infrastructures around the planet. Yergin explains how China produces 70% of the world's solar panels, surpassing Germany as the world's largest producer of solar panels in 2013. Cost reduction has made solar panels increasingly affordable with prices decreasing 85% between 2010 and 2019. Moreover, 2020 has seen the Chinese wind generated power market produce 'above the combined total for Europe, Africa, the Middle East and Latin America'. Therefore, while the architecture of achieving carbon neutrality lies with national governments, ultimately the technology that will get us there will be made in China.

Chinese authoritarianism provides the state with powers to enact measures that would be considered unthinkable in the West. For instance, when the state tried to bring China's coal energy mix down to 65% by 2017 from the 2012 level of 68.5% the chief administrator in Beijing decided to implement a total ban on coal. Shapiro and Li said 'in the face of horrendous pressure from multiple central level ministerial authorities, local officials were frightened into becoming environmental warriors'.

Re-forestation seems to be an area of celebration and success for the Chinese environmental movement. Li and Shapiro highlight how 'even nowadays tree planting remains the safest form of activism under authoritarianism. They explain how 70.5 billion trees have been planted in the last 4 decades, with China even having a national day for tree planting – March 12th – and a 1984 law which obliged every male aged 11 to 60 and every female from 11 to 55 to plant three to five trees per year. Nonetheless, Shapiro and Li warn about the low survival rates for many of these trees: 5% in Gansu and 34% in Beijing.

Chinese use of coal provides the greatest evidence that they are failing to meet the Paris Agreement goals. It is argued that in order to keep global warming below 1.5 degrees, 80% of coal needs to remain in the ground, however, China is 'adding three new highly efficient coal fired plants each month'. As cited earlier 60% of

China's energy comes from coal, moreover, the dirtiest of carbon emitting habits is being exported throughout the Silk Road. A 2019 study by Greenpeace East Asia indicates that China has put over five times more coal power into the Belt and Road Initiative than into Wind and Solar, moreover, 'China's commercial banks face few restrictions on funding coal fired plants' suggesting that China is ignoring what David Wallace Wells describes as 'carbon outsourcing' and with coal sites being built throughout the 131 Belt and Road countries, including in European sites like Bosnia and Herzegovina, Li and Shapiro accept 'the Chinese economy is unlikely to lose its coal addiction anytime soon'.

We have a situation where the technology for decarbonisation is made in China yet China is made on fossil fuels.

11th of August 2011

THE SIGNIFICANCE OF BRITISH FILM
IN THE CHINESE IMAGINATION

British knowledge of Chinese culture is dire. Chinese soft power is almost non-existent. China has given the world neither Coca Cola or Hollywood, however, it is through a shared appreciation of Western culture that Britain has a lot more in common with the Chinese collective imagination than one might imagine. Figures since 2010 demonstrate that films written by British authors, films set in Britain and films by British directors were consistently popular in China. Despite British liberalism being consistently antagonized by Chinese authoritarianism, it is likely the citizens in both countries derive energy from the dreams and visions demonstrated through British cinema. This level of cultural liberalism was prohibited in Stalinist Russia. Stalin used film to strengthen his cult of personality, removing Trotsky from Eisenstein's 1928 film *October* and banning some 37 films between 1935 and 1936. Therefore, the common experience of film should be utilised to build a common language between Britain and China to achieve future realities on a wide range of eventualities from environmental sustainability to nuclear warfare.

Christopher Nolan seems to be the most significant director in China. In 2010 *Inception* was the 3rd biggest film. In 2012, *The Dark Knight Rises* was the 7th biggest film. In 2014, *Inception* was the 4th biggest film. In 2020, *Interstellar* re-released as the 24th biggest film and *Inception* re-released as the 47th biggest film. Collectively Nolan films made approximately 264 million dollars at the Box Office, promoting themes on law and order through *The Dark Knight Rises*, Western Intelligence through *Inception* and climate disaster through *Interstellar.*

Like Britain, China has a mutual infatuation with the worlds created by JRR Tolkien and JK Rowling. In 2010 *Harry Potter and the Deathly Hallows Part One* was the 7th biggest film. In 2011, *Harry Potter and the Deathly Hallows Part Two* was the 3rd biggest film. In 2013, *The Hobbit: An Unexpected Journey* was the 20th biggest film. In 2014 *The Hobbit: The Desolation of Smaug* was the 17th biggest film. In 2020 the rerelease of *Harry Potter and the Philosopher's Stone* was the 19th biggest film. These alternative realities envisioned by JK Rowling and JRR Tolkien are arguably the two most popular in the modern collective British imagination. In my childhood, one was either experiencing the world through JK Rowling or JRR Tolkien. My entire imagination of the natural landscape was monopolised through the Lord of the Rings Trilogy.

Visions of Britain are not confined to the world of Dragons, Hobbits, Witches and Wizards. The Chinese seemingly show an infatuation with more quotidian and prosaic English films. In 2017, Torquay's very own Agatha Christie had a Box Office hit with *Murder on the Orient Express* being the 56th biggest film in China. *Paddington 2* was the 62nd biggest film. In 2018 the 62nd biggest film was Beatrix Potter's *Peter Rabbit* and the 63rd biggest film was Rowan Atkinson's *Johnny English Strikes Again*. Collectively these peculiarly British films made $115 million at the Chinese Box Office, emphasising the collective Chinese delight at stories that one associates with Chocolate Box Villages in May time Somerset.

Without yet mentioning James Bond - *Skyfall* and *Spectre* made $ 143 million dollars at the Chinese box office - it is clear that the powerful images of Britain found in film are shared by all the Chinese people that have enjoyed these same cultural artefacts. It is said Thomas Paine learnt the Bible by heart to effectively communicate ideas and stories with the masses. Whether in co-operation over climate or conversation over the pandemic, British film should create the foundation for effective communication with the Chinese, because, if we are able to collectively imagine the stories, characters and images in Nolan, Tolkien, Rowling,

Christie, Potter, Atkinson and Paddington, then we might have a good chance at moving to a language and world we all like to imagine.

4th of June 2021

PETER MORGAN: PLATFORM CAPITALISM'S RUDYARD KIPLING

Just as Stanley Kubrick translated 18th century paintings for film shots, such as William Hogarth's *Marriage A-La Mode* and John Constable's *Malvern Hall,* The Crown watches as if each scene is a painting from the Royal Academy. The Britain of The Crown is the Britain of the National Portrait Gallery, Rules Restaurant, the Royal Opera House and St Pauls. It is a joy to view these areas in high definition and have London's greatest spaces bought to life by its most famous family. My affection for the films of Eric Rohmer has created a pining for Britain to be captured with the same care and attention. Britons are not confined to the physical and etymological parameters that breed the intimacy of films like *Rayon Vert* and *Il Vitteloni*, and often our best and brightest get usurped by Hollywood. The Crown offers some of the Noveau Realist geist, yet it is American money invested in a story about royalty and thus fails to capture the quotidian charm, of say, French seaside towns in the summer. Moreover, just as these films have the arrogance of not expecting western viewers, every episode of The Crown is positioned as the opening of the London 2012 Olympics. These portraits are built to last and characterise.

Netflix is the world's largest platform streaming service. At the end of 2019, there were 183 million Netflix subscribers, a third of these were American. The Crown introduces the entire planet to many cultural and political figureheads that would otherwise be unknown. The Crown is the 21st century's most important tool for British historical memory. The political portraits in The Crown are likely to supplant a number of collective memories of 20th century British history and will undoubtedly be deployed in schools to stop yet another showing of Andrew Marr's *History of*

Modern Britain.

Through curating stories of Britain's most culturally significant family, Peter Morgan, the series creator, has become one of the country's most powerful writers. The significance of both writer and family is of great entertainment. The former's significance comes through the ability to design the imagination with the funds and reach of Netflix, the latter through their omnipresence within the historical collective conscience. Aside from Charlie Brooker, it is difficult to imagine a modern popular writer who has the ability to radically transform geopolitical institutions through storytelling. Whereas Shakespeare once dramatized dead monarchs to please the court of Queen Elizabeth, Morgan caricatures the present Royal Family to win favour amongst the emperors of Platform Capitalism. The Crown feels like Surveillance Capitalism's Elgin Marbles or Cleopatra's Needle with appropriations of former empires robbed, repurposed and distorted to legitimise modern ones.

What are the political impacts of Netflix's Rudyard Kipling? I fear The Crown has weakened the future of the Royal Family. The fourth season depicts an institution in which the most capable and commendable members, aside from Princess Anne, are from an older generation, and thus, the family get less likeable with age. This of course would lead to a conclusion that, beyond the Queen, the Royal Family has no significance in the 21st century. Prince Charles is represented queerly, in a manner similar to Bertie Wooster (with Camilla as Jeeves) or Alan Partridge (with Diana as Lynn). I would make the claim that Morgan uses The Crown to encourage Charles to abdicate, continually littering the series with question marks about accession, with Olivia Coleman's final speech probing whether Charles' *really* expects to be king. He does. Prince Harry, the only individual with the memory, experience and training to effectively support Prince William long term, has left the Royal Family. Given Megan Markel's line of work, his decision must in some way be influenced by Morgan's depictions. If The Crown fails to provide sufficient support to Prince William, either through lionisation or transforming Prince Charles' caricature, then the series can legitimately be described as a threat to the future of the Monarchy.

In the Empires of Platform Capitalism, the court Jester has become king. Morgan and his players are keen to enter the minds of collective historical memory to assure their position in the future, and yet, they will need to do more to protect the Royals or risk hurting the family they love to represent.

20th of November 2020

A LETTER TO AMERICA

Dear America,

I would like to write a letter to explain how the President appears to have transferred nationalism to the United Kingdom. This sense of Britain is delusional. Most effectively this can be shown through delegitimising Trump's major British supporters as either disingenuous or fame oriented.

First, I have to explain what it is like being British and growing up with the United States. From the moment you are born, you are bought up as an Anglo-American. In the first 7 years of my life The Simpsons, Lion King and Jurassic Park were three of my imagination's most important building blocks. I live by the River Thames and at parties between Putney Bridge and Hampton Court you would hear American Music; The Pharcyde, A Tribe Called Quest, Parliament, Kendrick Lamar. The outfits would be North Face, Nike and Patagonia. At home on Sundays, we played Frank Sinatra, Sam Cooke, Bob Dylan and Nina Simone. From the age of 14 to 16, I was obsessed with The Sopranos. From 16 to 18 it was Mad Men. My school was founded by Queen Elizabeth the First 222 years before American independence. The British education system is far more concerned with America than with Europe. At 16 we studied To Kill a Mockingbird and the American Civil Rights Movement. At 17 we studied The Great Gatsby. At 18 we studied the American political system. It is therefore natural that Britons care deeply about the state of America.

Donald Trump believes deeply in the special relationship. Trump's mother, Mary Anne MacLeod Trump, was born in the Outer Hebrides of Scotland. Trump reintroduced the Churchill bust, that had been replaced during the Obama administration with one of Martin Luther King Jr. Beyond speaking to Vladimir Putin, the most humbled Trump has ever seemed is when attending Buckingham Palace for the Royal Banquet, describing the Queen as a 'great great woman', Prince Charles as 'so good so good' and Harry as a 'really fine young man' adding 'I think the whole family is really terrific'.

Orwell argues that transferred nationalism allows the individual to be 'more vulgar, more silly, more malignant, more dishonest – than he could ever be on behalf of his native country, or any unit of which he had real knowledge' adding 'transferred nationalism, like the use of scapegoats, is a way of attaining salvation without altering one's conduct'. I would argue that Trump's adoration for the mother country seems like a misplaced attempt to inflate American nationalism. This can be found through Trump's conduct with the British peoples and policy decisions such as during Coronavirus when Trump banned travel from all countries aside from the United Kingdom. The problem is when we inspect Trump's British connection, contacts either seem contemptuous towards the President or significant purely through association with Trump.

Trump's most visible connections with Britons are Boris Johnson, Piers Morgan, Nigel Farage, Katie Hopkins and Raheem Kassam. Two of these have provided strong and damning condemnations of President Trump. Nigel Farage is keen to manipulate Donald Trump for political gain, whereas Katie Hopkins, one of the most hated people in Britain, and Raheem Kassam, virtually unknown in this country, are making careers out of supporting Trump.

Trump continually attempts to align himself with Boris Johnson. He has repeatedly referred to Johnson as 'Britain Trump'. When Johnson won the party leadership election Trump said, 'a really good man is going to be the prime minister of the UK'. Speaking to Nigel Farage in October he wrote 'Boris is the exact guy for the times. If you and he get together you would be an unstoppable force'. Boris Johnson, when he wasn't shackled by the need to secure a free trade agreement, described Trump as an individual of 'stupefying ignorance that makes him frankly unfit to hold the office of president of the United States'.

When Trump visited Britain for the State Banquet Piers Morgan was given an exclusive interview where they sentimentally remembered Trump watching the coronation in 1953, suggesting that the 2019 Royal Banquet may have been one of the greatest moments of his life. Despite these intimacies, Piers Morgan has now been unfollowed by Trump on Twitter following the former News of the World editor's description of Trump's handling of the Coronavirus as 'terrible' showing a 'complete inability to pivot to the kind of leadership you need in a crisis'.

Nigel Farage's relationship with Donald Trump, although far more genuine than Johnson or Morgan's feels somewhat exploitative with Farage using Trump as a platform to amplify his political strategies and goals, getting Trump to support a Brexit situation that the President doesn't understand. Farage's October 2019 interview with Trump watches like a fraudster who beams like a Cheshire cat, talking about the Queen to an elderly couple while they unknowingly give their bank details to someone who plans to empty their bank accounts.

Katie Hopkins and Raheem Kassam are quite clearly aligning themselves with Donald Trump so as to enjoy the fame that neither of them has ever enjoyed in the United Kingdom. During the Trump presidency, both have become regular figures on Fox News seemingly to act as representatives of British public opinion. Katie Hopkins, despite being well known through shows like The Apprentice and Celebrity Big Brother, has been politically insignificant before the association with Trump. Raheem Kassam, formerly Farage's chief political advisor, was virtually unheard of in the British media. His first performance that gained attention, beyond a Breitbart interview with Tommy Robinson, was the discussion with Newsnight about visiting Trump following his election victory, unsurprisingly his entire media presence seems to be an attempt to provide the illusion of British support for the

Trump presidency. Most Britons don't know who Raheem Kassam is.

Trump's transferred nationalism cannot be found in any of the places it claims to be. Boris Johnson thinks he is an idiot. He has broken up with Piers Morgan. He is left with an increasingly irrelevant Nigel Farage, and, in Katie Hopkins and Raheem Kassam, two fringe characters of the British media whose newfound fame seems to be based on the combination of supporting Donald Trump and the false notion that they are representative of British opinion. As for the Royals, Trump has confidently removed the United States from the Paris Climate Agreement which Prince Charles did so much to create. Trump, along with Kassam and Hopkins, is fooling voters into believing that he is a friend of the United Kingdom.

Trump has damaged our country. His transferred nationalism knows no roots. It is time America realise that they need to vote for a president who can do justice to the special relationship. Do not believe Trump's good words about Britain. Disregard British supporters like Hopkins and Kassam that pretend to be representative of British public opinion and gain all significance through support of Trump. Instead, remember how Trump has failed his nation and hurt British communities.

Best,

Sam Guinness

18th of July 2020

PRESIDENT BIDEN: THE AMERICAN DREAM RETURNS HOME

Donald Trump should never have happened. Trump's America, with monster trucks, dodgy casinos and WWE, displaced our American dreams. The America of *Highway 61, Deerhunter* and *To Kill a Mockingbird* could not have happened in the same society that was leaving the Paris Agreements, withdrawing from the Iran deal and divesting from the World Health Organization during the worst pandemic since the 1918 Spanish Flu. As Britons left for Berlin to escape Brexit, Americans came to Britain to escape Trump.

And yet, as Biden gave his inauguration speech, with Trump exiled to a golf course in Florida, I was flooded with American dreams. Bob Dylan, Frank Sinatra, Sam Cooke, Public Enemy, Captain Winters, The Beatles, The Rolling Stones, Martin Luther King, Franklin Roosevelt, Marlon Brando, Tony Soprano, Simba, Martin Scorsese, Quentin Tarantino, Brad Pitt, Miles Davies, Jimi Hendrix, Joan Holloway. The youthful fantasies that constructed my HBO Counter-Cultural imagination came back to me as reality. It was like in The Beatles' song *You Never Give Me Your Money* where Paul McCartney reviews how the band went from Merseyside clubs to global domination, singing *'one sweet dream came true/ pick up the bags get in the limousine'*. I've visited the ruins of the Beatles Ashram in Rishikesh. I'm aware it's nothing like *Within You Without You*, nonetheless, these illusions were strong enough to get my girlfriend and I to India. Christopher Hitchens recalls seeing James Baldwin warn Londoners that Nixon is 'your president too'. From climate change to cybersecurity, President Biden will galvanise and strengthen Western nations towards navigating our greatest problems. For the moment, I suggest that you pause, smile, and consume the video games, novels, records and films that built your American Dream. Realise, just as we all knew in World War Two, that Britain and the entirety of Europe can be saved by the United States of America.

21st of January 2021

BILLIE EILISH'S RADIO SHOW
IS A MASTERPIECE

From the beginning of humanity two of the most important features of our society have been family and music. Family and music survived the cognitive, agricultural and industrial revolution. Musician Billie Eilish and her Dad have created the perfect exhibition of the importance of family life and music. The Me and Dad Radio Show offers 6 hours and 30 minutes of discussion with the O'Connell Family covering meditations, memories and analysis of certain songs. Musicians featured include Radiohead, Christine Aguilera, Britney Spears, Mumford and Sons, Baxter Drury, Jorja Smith, Phoebe Bridges, The Beatles, The Rolling Stones.

I have met various Americans that have a natural attitude of responsibility and leadership. They exude a confidence tailored to being at the centre of the modern world. Traditionally the British aristocracy have been known to have possessed 'noblesse oblige', the sense that privilege demands leadership and responsibility. Orwell in 1941 wrote that the English ruling class were 'morally fairly sound' because they were always ready to be killed in a time of war. Absent of political discussion, the O'Connell family exhibit the confidence and intelligence we are seeking from the most powerful nation on the planet. They embody and communicate the idea and style of America that Trump did so much to destroy. Listening to these 6 radio shows, I'm flooded with memories of the America seen in documentary films like Gimme Shelter, Woodstock, The Beatles in America and The Last Waltz, televisions shows like Mad Men, and songs like Simon and Garfunkel's *America*, The Band's *The Weight* and The Doors' *LA*

Woman.

Patrick O'Connell, Billie's Dad, has a very good knowledge of music built from the foundation of The Beatles. His descriptions of America feel like the calmer parts of Scorsese and Tarantino, commenting on George Harrison's writing style and the cultural significance of Dean Martin.

Maggie Baird, Billie's mum, has a beautiful voice. She reminds me of the actress Sally Field. The songs she selects are intimately connected with family memories, telling a very lovely story of her father being in love with the singer Peggy Lee.

Finneas, Billie's Brother, has intelligence, esteem and confidence mixed with self deprecation and sincerity. Finneas' keen networking mind is demonstrated with the swagger of someone with great command of music and the industry.

And then we have Billie Eilish. She's got an incredible knowledge of culture, sounding like an individual who has spent thousands of hours watching MTV as a child. Billie's memory for lyrics is great. Her command and appreciation of the English language is beautiful. She's sarcastic and witty in her word play, applied in conversation and in the deconstruction of selected songs that she often harmonises and sings with.

The collective imagination is built from our musical memories of California, New York, London and Paris. We lust for the princes and princesses that make our dream reality. We want Lana Del Ray, the Strokes and Frank Sinatra from New York, David Bowie and The Clash from London, Edith Piaf and Serge Gainsbourg from Paris and now in California, we want The Beach Boys, The Doors and Billie Eilish.

The great American stories on family are very often concerned with the Mafia, like in the Godfather and the Sopranos, or ridicule, as with The Simpsons and Family Guy. These radio shows are a masterpiece. The O'Connell's are performers and orators. They are a family with good connection to one another, communicated through a love and affection for music.

6th of April 2022

IT'S COMING HOME: ENGLISH FOOTBALL AND THE IMPORTANCE OF SONG

The England versus Denmark match in the semi-finals of the European Championship demonstrated the importance of song. The national anthem has the same symbolic significance as swearing on the Bible in court. The words of the anthem are sung not to exhibit the singing talent of the footballers but to have the footballers give their commitment to the nation and the fans. It is a singing pledge that demonstrates that these players identify the same tune, the same queen and the same country as the crowds in the stadium and the spectators at home. After the game, the Skinner and Baddiel song *'it's coming home'* is sung by the players and fans in the stadium and then throughout London until the early hours of Thursday morning. It seemed to act as the identity badge that transformed London into a theme park for all that were willing to celebrate England's victory. In the midst of the carnival, it seems the meaning of 'it's coming home' has been forgotten or repurposed. Forgotten, because the term 'football's coming home' said directly as a response to England's progression in the tournament is a misinterpretation of the lyrics. 'It's coming home' was written in reference to the 1996 European competition where football was 'coming home' because England, the birthplace of football, was hosting the tournament. The lyrics then go on to talk about the difficulty and excitement of watching England over the years then going on to explain the hopes of Baddiel and Skinner - 'I know that (The 1966 World Cup victory) was then but it could be again'. In another way, 'it's coming home' seems to be the anthem celebrating the end of Covid, with 'it' being the excited hedonism found on the streets of London where people smile, eyes glazed over with four pints of draught lager shouting 'it's coming home' like Ebenezer Scrooge shouting 'MERRY CHRISTMAS' on Christmas Day.

While the majority who watch don't play football, they are able to shout and sing and the song creates a collective consciousness through tone, delivery and the images created through the song's lyrics. After over a year of isolation, it is an extraordinary thing to share a space and song and greeting with our fellow man.

A song is an instrument of collective communication that provides an insight on how we view the world. The lords of song, Frank Sinatra, Elvis, Ella Fitzgerald, Leonard Cohen, Mick Jagger and Alex Turner became an identity in themselves:

Frank Sinatra is an actor who defines wealth, his songs and his voice are, in themselves, an explanation of the good life. For many, Elvis was and always will be the definition of America. Through April in Paris, Ella Fitzgerald can articulate and create the most accurate feeling of what it is that people enjoy about Paris. Some think Leonard Cohen is the author of the book on love and that Mick Jagger's the definition of Rock and Roll. Alex Turner, for my generation, was the main architect for our urban attitude of wit and confidence. These singers are Western Gods. They have given one of the only explanations for the meaning of life. Their existence and representation is the realisation of our fantasy, the articulation and performance of the energy that we seek.

12th of July 2021

BAND OF BROTHERS AND
THE ENDURING INFLUENCE
OF ADOLF HITLER

One could build the image of masculinity through the images and themes communicated through Band of Brothers. In many ways, my friends and I are the male products of a litany World War Two films, television programmes, video games and afternoons spent playing with toy machine guns as children. In Britain, the story of World War Two is the great moral story that one learns at a very early age. Entire afternoons are spent at the Imperial War Museum and war memorials are very often the central features in towns or schools. The most masterful communication of the events on the Western Front are told through Band of Brothers. This HBO/BBC drama features the true story of the Easy Company of the 101st Airborne Division as they get parachuted into Normandy and then fight through France, Holland and Austria. In 2021 I rewatched Band of Brothers for the first time since 2010, when the KGS Hockey B-team drove through Wageningen, Holland, pretending to be the allies liberating the Western front as we watched it on our portable DVD players. Through studying World War Two one is made aware of the strangeness surrounding the conditions for war. Band of Brothers is a story about men who were driven to fight for their lives because of a host of historical factors that took place before they were born.

It is strange that so many of our common images of community and historical memory and masculinity and adventure are a consequence of Hitler because Hitler is arguably one of the strangest characters History has ever known. The fanatical megalomaniacal insanity of Hitler is well documented by two of World War Two's greatest chroniclers. George Orwell wrote of Hitler 'people who say that Hitler is Antichrist, or alternatively, the Holy Ghost, are nearer an understanding of the truth than the intellectuals who for ten dreadful years have kept it up that he is merely a figure out of comic opera, not worth taking seriously'. Hannah Arendt writes that Hitler once explained to the supreme commanders of the Wehrmacht that he was 'irreplaceable' and that 'the destiny of the Reich depends on me alone'. Writing 60 years later Christopher Hitchens provides a perfectly arranged summary asserting that 'Germany was governed by an ultra-rightist, homicidal, paranoid maniac who had begun by demolishing democracy in Germany itself, who believed that his fellow countrymen were a superior race and who attributed the evils in the world to a Jewish conspiracy'.

It's bizarre to imagine how much of our present culture stems from a hated lunatic. Without Hitler, the statues of Churchill in Parliament Square, Bomber Harris outside St Clements, the Animals outside of Hyde Park and the Blitz opposite the London Eye wouldn't exist. The Barbican, Call of Duty 2 or World At War, Saving Private Ryan, Schindler's List, Inglorious Bastards, Fury, Downfall, Great Escape, Band of Brothers, lessons on the Holocaust, we would have none of it.

Regardless of how much moral credibility we are to extract from studying Hitler and the Nazi's, the fact of the matter is that the reaction towards the Nazi's created the directors of 20th century geopolitics, the architects of our European cities and the playmasters of the European theatrics that defined 21st century liberalism and the subject of our cultures most prized pieces of work.

Today one of the major political consequences of World War Two is that it created the conditions for the CCP to take China from the Western supported Nationalist government. Without delving into the counterfactual fates of the Soviet Union, the British Empire and Fascist Japan, we have a direct correlation between our present state of affairs with China and the actions of Hitler. Whether we like it or not, we are still living in and as a consequence of Hitler's imagination.

4th of December 2021

SAVING THE EUROPEAN UNION: THE CLIMATE REFUGEE CRISES AND THE FAR RIGHT

Since graduating from the education system, the experience of human cowardice is one of the subjects that fascinates me the most. Through virtue of fear, ignorance or misconception, people actively attempt to ignore certain subjects. In some cases, people invest energy in political ideologies or ideas simply to avoid answering questions or having debates on given subjects. Very often this aversion towards conversations that seek to solve problems leads to the creation of living standards that actively harm the individual and the community in both the short and long term, nonetheless, they have on some level kept face through virtue of failing to interact with rationality and logic – undeniably two of the most dangerous principles to protect if you are concerned with not hurting people's feelings.

Europe's most insidious new subject is the question of immigration. If the European Union fails to implement an effective migration policy, then Europe will fall to the far right. The far right is keen to have the European Union destroyed. Unlike the British Conservative Party, Marine Le Pen of the National Front, Matteo Salvini of the Five Star movement and Viktor Orban have all been courting Putin. Marine Le Pen has previously received a 9 million euro loan thanks to Putin. Similarly, it is Putin's greatest western benefactor Donald Trump who has tried to align his movement with characters like Le Pen, Orban and Salvini. If you don't believe me watch *The Brink* a documentary in which Bannon travels around Europe offering empty support to whoever's seen as the far right candidate in whatever European capital. We're not talking about conspiracy. We have a very clear and transparent alignment between pro-

Putin political movements in Europe and America that aim to destroy the European Union and likely weaken the NATO alliance. Beyond this, Trump demonstrates how right-wing populism can manipulate the democratic system into electing people that aren't ready for the intellectual challenges of governance, warfare and diplomacy.

The far right took advantage of the Refugee crises in which Refugees from Syria, Iraq and Afghanistan attempted to enter Europe. By 2016 nearly 5.2 million refugees reached European shores. The impact of the Refugee crisis was explicit throughout Europe in the summer of 2015 and 2016. In 2015, I went travelling on trains from Greece to Berlin often crowded with Syrian refugees. At an Athens train station, a Greek journalist told me that Greece was going to be sending all the refugees to Germany in retaliation for mistreatment during the Greek government debt crisis. In 2016, I was surprised by how far Refugees were travelling. Going to a film that supported Refugee integration in Dortmund, Refugees were very evident through the city centre, after the film I met two Afghan refugees and one Nigerian. Freddy, a Nigerian Refugee and massive Liverpool fan, illustrated his journey saying 'they told me that there were tigers but I survived the tigers'.

There is a correlation between the migrant crises, anti-immigration policies and the rise of the Far Right. In France in 2017 Marine Le Pen's National Front, a party that couldn't even secure funding from French banks because of ties with anti-semitism, received 33.90% of the vote. 4 years before she had received 17.9% of the vote. In Italy, the countries right wing populist leader reached the position of Deputy Prime Minister in 2018, his support, according to the BBC, a result of anti-immigration policies following a 'big influx of sub-Saharan migrants from North Africa in 2016'. In 2017, two years after Merkel offered asylum to a million refugees, the country who has done more than anyone else to remember the legacy of totalitarianism gave 12.6% of votes to the AfD gaining, 94 seats.

In Spain in 2019 Vox won 52 seats. Prior to 2019, 'just a single seat had been won by a far right candidate' since the death of dictator Francisco Franco. This was in 1979. In Austria in 2017 the Freedom Party became the only far right party in power, just like Italy, France, Germany and Spain, immigration and the migrant crises were voters' greatest concerns.

The European Union has to make serious preparations in anticipation for a huge influx of climate refugees or risk the end of the European Union. The IPCC predicts there will be 200 million climate refugees by 2050 because of ecological changes that make parts of our world totally uninhabitable. The Groundswell project predicts that the climate refugee crises created in Sub-Saharan Africa, Latin America, and the rest of South Asia will be ten times worse than the Syrian migration crisis with 140 million refugees in 2050. In 2012, it was predicted in Bangladesh that 3 to 10 million people would be forced to relocate over the next 40 years because of climate change. My conversation with Freddy in Dortmund demonstrates that, be they from Africa or the Middle East, when refugees are met with disaster they look towards the European Union. If Europe doesn't prevent mass migration into its Liberal Empire then Europe's Liberal Empire will be destroyed and rebuilt in the image of authoritarians like Vladimir Putin.

We are 28 years away from the IPCC prediction of 200 million climate refugees. The 2022 French Presidential election offers an important case study on the importance of migration for the future of European politics. Of the four leading Presidential candidacies, two are from the right and two are from the far right. Of those challenging Emanuel Macron, Immigration is the defining feature of the centre-right campaign of Valerie Pecresse and the two far right campaigns of Eric Zemmour and Marine Le Pen. The EU have to make plans today to stop mass migration determining Europe's political future.

9th of January 2022

MANUEL CASTELLS AND THE PHENOMENAL COMMUNICATIVE POWER OF THE BBC

Manuel Castells' book *Communicative Power* provides a theory of the communicative power of media organisations. Castells writes that 'power is primarily exercised by the construction of meaning in the human mind through processes of communication enacted in global/local multimedia networks of mass communication, including self-communication'. In light of the Convervative government's decision to remove some £2 billion pounds of funding from the BBC over the next six years, it is important that we are able to conceptualise the significance of the BBC to the local, national and international media. The ideas found in Castells' communicative power exemplify the extraordinary success of the BBC in accumulating communicative and network power. Moreover, the removal of £2 billion pounds would serve to damage the quality of content created, damage the BBC's reputation as the world's leading independent broadcaster, weaken the BBC's position as the world's most popular site for international news, weaken the companies networking power, reduce the amount of UK focused content, damage the BBC's position as a gatekeeper, erode a sense of British national identity and reduce the United Kingdom's communicative power.

Significance of the BBC within the Modern Media Infrastructure

Manuel Castells illustrates three major factors that explain the BBC's significance within the global media infrastructure. Firstly, Castells stresses the BBC's tradition and reputation as the world's greatest independent broadcaster. Secondly, Castell's emphasises the BBC's ability to set the international news agenda. Thirdly, Castells talks about the importance of a Media organisation's ability to build networks.

Castells stresses that the independence of the BBC is of central importance towards its success writing that 'the BBC has been hailed around the world as a model of a public corporation asserting its independence from direct government interference, although some acts by the Blair government tarnished this image without destroying the reputation of the BBC as a reference for independent public media around the world.'. Therefore, Castells says that the BBC is one of the world's greatest independent media organisations in part because the BBC isn't politicised by the government. The Government's attempts to withdraw funding from the BBC on account of their 'very-left wing, often hypocritical and frequently patronising views', demonstrate the Government actively attempting to politicise the BBC hence abusing the company's independence. Given that the BBC has built conditions that have allowed the largely right-wing movement of Brexit, and then, the election of the largest Tory government since 1979, the accusation of Britain's largest media organisation being left-wing is devoid of evidence. In turn, from my experience working with Extinction Rebellion, I am aware that the BBC are routinely subject to a lot of criticism for being right-wing. Therefore, the government's attempts at political government interference and withdrawal of £2 billion pounds of funding over the next six years, threaten the BBC's capability and reputation as one of the world's greatest independent media organisations.

The BBC is an extraordinary asset to the United Kingdom. Castells' book emphasises that one of the greatest powers the BBC provides Britain is the ability to set the international news agenda. Castells writes that 'studies by Van Belle and Golan demonstrate that 'global media' corporations depend on key elite publications (that they do not own) to set their news agendas.'. Castells includes the BBC, along with The New York Times, Al Jazeera and The Economist as the key towards setting the international news agenda. This gives the BBC the editorial power of selecting which news is worth reading and how to frame the world's most important news stories. Smaller organisations throughout the planet, Golan gives the examples of CBS, NBC and ABC in regard to The New York Times, will then follow the BBC's editorial and framing decisions. The communicative power accumulated by the BBC and therefore the British people can be measured in part through the popularity of the news website. Writing in 2009, Castells mentions that the BBC is the most visited news web on the planet being visited by 'over 46 million visitors per month, 60% originating from outside the UK', 11 years later and the BBC is still the world's most popular news site with 1.1 billion visitors in December 2021. The communicative power obtained by the BBC is by no means guaranteed. While The Daily Mail (375.2 million visitors in December 2021) and The Guardian (302.5 million visitors in December 2021) offer very impressive agenda setting capabilities, the BBC is more than three times more popular than them both. To have an independent state funded news site that is more popular than every other media organisation on the planet, MSN, CNN, Google, The New York Times, India Times and Buzzfeed, is extraordinary and comparable to America's greatest companies like Google, Facebook and Microsoft. As a publicly owned British Broadcaster the BBC may well be the world's claim to the spiritual home of the English Language. The withdrawal of £2 billion pounds over the next six years, for political excuses without evidence, will serve to dilute Britain's greatest engine of communicative power and weaken our nation. Following the infrastructural domination of Internet monopolies and the political result of Brexit, it is absurd that we would think about divesting in our greatest source of communicative power particularly when we have been so impotent in conceptualising the problems created and the power devolved to major Silicon Valley Technology Companies.

Much of the BBC's significance to the world's media infrastructure is based on the companies' infrastructural and social network. Castells writes about the networking conditions needed to build a successful media organisation: 'media networks do not exist in a vacuum. Their success is dependent on their ability to successfully leverage connections to other critical networks in finance, technology, cultural industries, advertising industries, suppliers of content, regulatory agencies, and political crises at large.' And that 'connections to writers, actors, performers, and other creative professionals are also essential for the success of media business. In the United States alone, the network of agents for artists, athletes and entertainers is a $6 billion a year industry'. The BBC has managed to build profoundly successful networks through local, national and international networks. They have the ability to train and attract the best media talent building some of the world's strongest media networks. The strength of the BBC's social networking is well demonstrated through music. BBC Radio 1's Big Weekend has managed to bring the world's biggest musicians to some of the most prosaic and unlikely areas of the United Kingdom. Radio 1's Big Weekend bought Billie Eilish to Middlesborough, Rihanna to Bangore and Bruno Mars to Derry. The BBC's radio presenters and music infrastructure, not adversely effected by the need to secure advertising revenue, have allowed them to experiment with DJs that are willing to pioneer new Artists, helping launch the careers of Britain's biggest stars like Ed Sheeran, Little Sims, George Ezra, Florence and the Machine, The Glass Animals, Bombay Bicycle Club and Loyle Carner, whilst also helping popularise and define entire music genres like Grime and Dubstep. In 2019 the UK music industry was worth £5.8 billion to the United Kingdom and music tourism is responsible for adding £4.7 billion. The BBC, due to its communicative power, infrastructural and social networks, is arguably the United Kingdom's most important platform for the safeguarding and continuation of this multibillion-pound industry. Withdrawing £2 billion pounds from the BBC in the next six years may well serve to weaken these networks, creating losses of billions of pounds for other industries in the United Kingdom.

The Importance of the BBC's Business Model Towards its Communicative Power

Castells highlights two ideas that explain the communicative power of the BBC: Firstly, the BBC's position as a broadcaster was created for and funded by the British people. Secondly, the importance of the BBC's protection from the pursuit of advertising funds.

Unlike Cadbury, Jaguar Land Rover and Asda, the BBC is a British company which is owned by the people of the United Kingdom. This is of great importance because it acts as a normative incentive toward the strengthening of local, national and international British connections and prioritises and harnesses British talent, be it musicians, writers, journalists, broadcasters, actors or directors. The BBC builds infrastructure with the view of building the whole nation. By contrast, Castells highlights that many major national media organisations are owned by foreign media conglomerates. For instance, Murdoch and News Corporation, founded in Australia, make 53% of its revenue from the United States and 32% from Europe. Some of Europe's largest national media organisations are owned by 'multiple corporations from multiple nations'. Germany's Vox is 49.5% owned by News Corporation, France's Canal Plus is 24.9% owned by News Corporation and Germany's Bertelsmann owned 24.9% by News Corporation. Were the BBC to be privatised in any way it would have to adapt its business model towards foreign companies and foreign interests thus compromising the focus on training and publicising the UK's best talent and attracting and building the UK's strongest media networks, thus, eroding the nation's character, identity and communicative power.

Castells emphasis on the importance of television in creating a national identity, emphasises the harm Nadine Dorries' policy threatens to the UK. Castells describes work by Tubella that 'has shown the decisive importance of television in constructing national identity under the conditions of cultural domination by another nation, as revealed by the important example of Catalan television in Spain after the post-Franco democratic regime'. The BBC's superior ability in comparison with platforms like Netflix and Amazon to offer content that focuses on the United Kingdom and creates a sense of national identity is demonstrated through the House of Common's select committee report on The Future of Public Service Broadcasting which found that 'in 2019, public service broadcasters provided approximately 32,000 hours of UK originated content, whereas Netflix and Amazon Prime combined provide 164 hours'. Therefore, the removal of funding will weaken the BBC's ability to make high quality British content and encourage viewers to replace British television and British culture with whatever the American streaming services provide.

One of the greatest advantages towards the BBC's license fee subscription model is that it protects the company from the relentless effort of pursuing advertising funds. Castells writes that 'Advertising is the backbone of global and local media business networks. Thus, it is present everywhere, in all cultural patterns and uses all platforms, from television and radio to the internet and mobile phones. It is through advertising that the culture of commodification, at the heart of global capitalism, influences all cultural expressions and their media support'. The BBC is protected from the uglier sides of the market through public ownership. This gives the BBC the ability to make more adventurous, creative, and frankly, better content. Dependence on advertising funds would strategize the BBC advertising model towards creating content through websites, podcasts, television, music, radio, sport and film that generates the most amount of attention. This attention would then get monitored, quantified and sold to advertisers as behavioural data. Given that the BBC media infrastructure is central to the creative and governance infrastructure of the United Kingdom a reliance upon advertising funds may serve to destroy this national infrastructure. Areas of the BBC that provide crucially important functions may fail to attract enough attention. In pursuit of advertising funds, we may never have heard Dubstep, Grime, Ed Sheeran, Little Simz or Loyle Carner. In pursuit of advertising funds, we may never have seen The Office, I May Destroy You, Killing Eve or People Just Do

Nothing. In pursuit of advertising funds, the songs and stories that have changed or defined people's lives may have never been created. In pursuit of advertising funds, Britain may have never built their own culture and, naturally, just been America's biggest fan.

The BBC's independence is ensured through safety from the state and safety from the market. The permanence and consistency of the license fee has given the BBC a hundred years to perfect and adapt the media ecosystem developing and upholding the highest standards of normative media goals like truthfulness, accuracy, objectivity, impartiality, fairness and public accountability. The BBC sets the tone for the rest of the world's media infrastructure. The BBC is powerful throughout the world because it produces high quality content, upholding and setting the moral and ethical standards of the media landscape.

Conclusion

Manuel Castells book Communicative Power accentuates that the BBC is one of if not the world's greatest media organisations. The communicative power accumulated through the BBC is of central importance towards Britain's local, national and international identity and reputation. Safeguarded from foreign ownership and advertising investment, the BBC has the safety to experiment with contemporary culture, pioneering music genres, musicians, television, film and journalism, at the same time as setting the normative ethical standards for the world's media. The government's attempts at politicisation and divestment will serve to deathly weaken our nation in a variety of ways. The English language is surely our country's greatest export and the BBC may well be its spiritual home.

5th of February 2022

ORATORICAL ABILITY AND COMMUNICATIVE POWER: HITLER, CHURCHILL, THE BEATLES, DONALD TRUMP, SAM HARRIS AND THE BBC

Even in times of great technological development, times of the radio, times of cinema, times of television, times of the smartphone and times of the algorithm, an individual Homo sapien has the ability to accumulate extraordinary amounts of communicative power. In the last one hundred years, oratorical talent has been responsible for many of the greatest accumulations of individual communicative power. Through examples like Hitler, Churchill, The Beatles and Donald Trump, we have seen the extraordinary influence of oratorical talent amidst our communications infrastructures.

Hitler's capacity for giving speeches and then utilising propaganda like radio and film permitted someone Orwell described as a 'criminal lunatic' to use the greatest products of science to introduce irrational political ideas from the Dark Ages. Hitler's speeches allowed a lonely unknown failed Austrian artist to capture the attention of the German audience, radio, newspapers and films to generate support and interest in ideas like global conspiracies of Jews and Bolsheviks. Viktor Klemperer, a Jewish German Philologist, wrote an excellent set of diaries throughout World War Two. He emphasised the importance of the radio in the success of Hitler, writing on the 14th of September 1933: 'pay attention to the role of *radio*! Not like other technical achievements: new content, new philosophy. But: new style. Printed matters suppressed. Oratorical, oral. Primitive – at a higher level.'. Klemperer suggests that the technology of radio served to enhance the communication of 'primitive' ideas, perhaps in part because it widened the audience that could assimilate information from politicians, accurately transmitting emotion through sound and capturing the attention of parts of society who may not have been reading the newspapers. Klemperer emphasises the paradoxical situation in which greater scientific development had led to peculiarly backwards political traditions. Klemperer wrote on the 31st of January in 1937: 'such tremendous things are being created, radio, aeroplane, sound film, and the most insane stupidity, primitiveness and bestiality cannot be eradicated – all invention results in murder and war'. Orwell makes a similar point criticising the Scientific Deterministic view of HG Wells writing in 1941, 'the order, the planning, the State encouragement of science, the steel, the concrete, the aeroplanes, are all there, but all in the service of ideas appropriate to the Stone Age. Science is fighting on the side of superstition'. Klemperer suggests that it is the technological development of the radio, that has created such conditions of political barbarism writing that 'for me radio destroys every form of religion and at the same time gives rise to religion. Gives rise to it twice over: a) because such a miracle exists b) because the human intellect invents, explains, makes use of it. But this same human intellect puts up with the Hitler government'. Therefore, Hitler's utilisation of the radio gave him the ability to accumulate the communication power to manipulate and bend all other technologies to his will evoking audience emotions described by Orwell as 'racial pride, leader worship, religious belief' and love of war'.

Similarly, Churchill applied his masterful oratorical skill to encourage bravery and resistance towards the Nazi's. As early as 1934, Churchill broadcast a speech on the BBC where he warned of war, claiming that 'there is a nation which has abandoned all its liberties in order to augment its collective might. There is a nation which with all its strength and virtues is in the grip of a group of ruthless men preaching a gospel of intolerance and racial pride, unrestrained by law, by Parliament or by public opinion'. Andrew Roberts emphasises the importance of Churchill's oratorical talents throughout Occupied Europe writing how 'in those cities and later across Occupied Europe, listening to Churchill's broadcasts over the radio became punishable by death, yet still people listened, because he could provide that one thing that tortured populations needed more than anything else: hope'. In networking terms, the invention of the radio allowed a single voice or node to become the central figure in communication with thousands or millions of other nodes. Therefore, the radio enhanced the power of these individuals, permitting them to introduce ideas and storylines that would then get adopted and enacted by citizens, families, communities and nations.

Nineteen years after Hitler shot himself in Berlin, John Lennon, Paul McCartney, George Harrison and Ringo Starr would demonstrate the power of oratorical magic through the gift of song. In 1964, four working-class lads from Liverpool, between the ages of 20 and 23, became the most famous people on the planet and were mobbed by thousands as they landed at JFK airport in New York. The Beatles weren't expecting the reaction, with George Harrison commenting that 'we heard our records were selling well in America, but it wasn't until we stepped off the plane... that we understood what was going on'. Lennon and McCartney's ability to write and deliver songs created emotions of love, excitement and pining. Audiences very often attribute the beauty of a singer's voice and the songs meaning exclusively towards the singer. Therefore, when The Beatles were singing *Please Please Me* and *Love Me Do*, it was as if their voice was the origin of love. What's more through the dissemination of these mini monologues through records and radio's they create a collective experience, where they become the source of love for millions, moreover, those millions then consolidate this form of love through communal enjoyment of The Beatles. The Beatles were not confined to the creation of pop records and between them, they introduced radical ideas into the Post-War world including experimentation with drugs, anti-war movements, climate protest through concert, and meditation. Since 1945, the musicians that have achieved the greatest levels of communicative power, David Bowie, Bruce Springsteen and Rihanna, are always popular singers. Therefore, it might be argued that the oratorical ability to sing is the foundation from which this communicative power is built. The radio plays, the television performances and the social media followers are all based on the individuals singing ability which is then transformed into communicative power through fame.

Despite having little intelligence or diplomatic skill, Donald Trump used his oratorical powers to defeat every candidate in the Republican Party primaries and then defeat Hillary Clinton in the 2016 Presidential Election. Whereas Hitler relied primarily on speeches and films to introduce dangerous ideas toward mainstream democracy, Trump's idiotic political positions are supported through his ability to perform with humour, energy and confidence on television, social media and radio. In the age of the attention economy, media and social media firms in part make money through capturing the attention of readers and generating behavioural data which companies can then sell to advertisers. Facebook and Google make around 90% of their profits through advertising tailored to behavioural data. Trump's ability to evoke shock and outrage was excellent for the attention economy. The right-wing praised his bolshiness. The left-wing published and condemned, social media and media companies made money through capturing the public's attention on television and social media. In turn, Trump's oratorical performances, the jokes, the stupidity and the fear, created free publicity that would've been the equivalent of hundreds of millions of pounds of digital advertising.

The mobile phone is the most addictive substance we own. Johan Harr writes that the average phone time of Americans is 3 hours 15 minutes. Given these figures, one might say that we are addicted to or dependent upon the smartphone or computers. If one is addicted to these products, they are likely to be amused by content that stimulates attention. These sensations might serve to satisfy the internet users' addiction, especially if they provide momentary transcendence from the repetition of work routines. I believe it is within this mental environment that the world got addicted to Trump. Even if we were addicted to hating Trump, he had gotten inside of our adrenal systems and therefore won the favour of the algorithm generating extraordinary levels of political advertising. Through Trump's oratorical performances he managed to make enough content to addict media and social media into following his every word. Trump's oratorical performances created conditions in which a far right candidate with little institutional support could defeat the Republican Party candidates and then Hilary Clinton in order to hold the most powerful democratic political position on the planet. This is probably the most alarming and powerful example since Hitler of how oratorical talent can be used to manipulate the communications infrastructure. In the age of AI, the algorithm, social media and electric cars America managed to elect a president who encouraged the US's greatest adversary, Vladimir Putin, to manipulate the democratic process and in the presence of epidemiology experts suggested that people could defeat coronavirus through injecting themselves with disinfectant.

Today, it is the podcast, which provides the most effective platform for the effective dissemination and synchronisation of information. Podcasts provide hosts a space to think and talk through problems and subjects in great depth. Instead of being confined to a weekly or daily radio slot episodes are delivered to subscribers' smartphones and laptops for free. The quality and convenience of information provided through podcasts are great. Throughout the Trump candidacy, Sam Harris employed the Making Sense podcast to lead the resistance against Donald Trump. Since 2016 Sam Harris dedicated at least 18 podcasts to the problems of Donald Trump and how to defeat him. These included conversations with the likes of General Stanley McChrystal, Gary Kasparov, Cass Sunstein, Andrew Marantz,

Preet Bahara, David Frum, Anne Applebaum and Andrew Sullivan. Harris used his masterful command of memory, social networks, conversational style and manipulation of language to offer constant commentary on the events of the Trump presidency exposing Trump's incapability, rudeness, stupidity and recklessness, helping coordinate and mobilise an effective response from voters and thinkers.

In conclusion, technological development has not disempowered the influence of the individual. The desire for individuals with the oratorical ability to communicate ideas and narratives that provide a meaning for our existence is relentless. Certain talented orators have the ability and luck to become individual supernodes within the communications network, using technologies like radio, television, the iPod and social media to disseminate and amplify their worldview. The consequences of this power are varied and extreme. Hitler used the radio to build a new religion of racial supremacy. Churchill used the radio to destroy Nazi Fascism. The Beatles disseminated their oratorical talents through records, the radio and television to be the genesis of love in the 1960s. Donald Trump got people addicted to his crazy oratorical performances through the mobile phone and the computer, arguably the two most addictive tools known to humankind. Sam Harris used the podcast to monitor, conceptualise and mobilise in opposition to the trauma of the Trump presidency.

Become aware of the songs, the speeches and the debates that are assimilated into your mind. Think about the communicative power of the individual that has delivered them. They may be in the process of transforming our planet.

30th of January 2022

Printed in Great Britain
by Amazon

85926793R00068